Matthew
The Hebrew Gospel

VOLUME I
(MATTHEW 1-8)

A Commentary by
Carroll Roberson

Publishing

Published by
Innovo Publishing, LLC
www.innovopublishing.com
1-888-546-2111

Providing Full-Service Publishing Services for
Christian Authors, Artists & Organizations: Hardbacks, Paperbacks,
eBooks, Audiobooks, Music & Videos

MATTHEW, THE HEBREW GOSPEL
Copyright © 2011 by Carroll Roberson
All rights reserved.

No part of this publication may be reproduced, stored in a retrieval system, or transmitted in any form or by any means electronic, mechanical, photocopying, recording, or otherwise, without the prior written permission of the author.

Scripture is taken from the King James Version of the Bible.

ISBN 13: 978-1-936076-63-5
ISBN 10: 1-936076-63-2

Cover Design & Interior Layout: Innovo Publishing, LLC

Printed in the United States of America
U.S. Printing History

First Edition: February 2011

Table of Contents

An Introduction to Matthew's Gospel 1

Chapter One 7

Chapter Two 19

Chapter Three 35

Chapter Four 49

Chapter Five 71

Chapter Six 95

Chapter Seven 111

Chapter Eight 123

Conclusion 141

An Introduction to Matthew's Gospel

The Old Testament scriptures end on a sad note. There were:

1) Unexplained Ceremonies
2) Unachieved Purposes
3) Unappeased Longings
4) Unfulfilled Prophecies

Between the Old and New Testaments are almost four hundred long years of silence. No prophet thundered and no king from the house of David sat on the throne in Jerusalem. Israel was a stranger in her own land except for about 100 years of the Hasmonean Dynasty (140–37 BC).

After the Babylonian captivity, the Israelites had learned their lesson about idolatry, and they had returned to the land of Israel under the permissive decrees of Cyrus and his successors. The temple worship had been reestablished, although the temple was in the hands of the corrupt Sadducees, who were mere puppets of Rome. Around 198 BC, under the Syrian ruler Antiochus the Great, the land of Israel was divided into the five provinces that we read about in the gospel accounts: Galilee, Samaria, Judaea, Trachonitis, and Perea (land beyond Jordan).

Among all of this political and religious trouble, the Person of the Messiah entered the world! Matthew alludes to the Old Testament scriptures over sixty times. And when Jesus the Christ taught the scriptures, He taught Himself from the Old Testament, or the *Tanakh* (**Luke 24:27, 44**). So this is why the gospel of Matthew is so important to our understanding the scriptures as a whole. The best commentary on the Bible is the Bible itself. So my desire is not to give you just another commentary, but to help you better understand the text from the historical, Hebrew perspective.

In my research over the years, the precious Lord has allowed me to uncover many wonderful, and sometimes unusual truths that I would like to share with you. I have been favored to travel to Israel many times over the years, and this has driven me to study ancient Jewish resources, historians, and early church fathers, as well as a deeper look inside the gospel accounts.

The gospel according to Matthew is unique, giving us the very first account of Jesus when we open the pages of the New Testament. Matthew, *Mattityahu*, (gift of Yahweh), was one of the gospel writers who actually walked with Christ himself. He was an eyewitness! He could have said, "I was there when it all happened." Another reason I have chosen Matthew's gospel is because it is documented by many of the early church fathers that Matthew wrote his gospel in the Hebrew dialect first, before it was ever translated into Greek. Here are a few examples:

"Now Matthew made an ordered arrangement of the oracles in the Hebrew language, and each translated it as he was able."
—Papias, Bishop of Heiropolis (60–130 AD)

"Matthew, also among the Hebrews, published a written gospel in their own dialect when Peter and Paul were preaching in Rome and founding the church there."
—Irenaeus, Bishop of Lyons (130–200 AD)

"Having learned by tradition concerning the four gospels, which are alone indisputable in the church of God under heaven, that there was written first that which is according to Matthew, who was once a publican, but was afterward an apostle of Jesus Christ, and it was issued to those who once were Jews but had believed, and was composed in Hebrew."
—Origen, Christian Theologian, Alexandria, Egypt (184–254 AD)

"Matthew, committed his gospel to writing in his native tongue"
—Eusebius, Bishop of Caesarea (263–339 AD).

It is also recorded that Saint Jerome, (347–420 AD), believed that the true way to study the gospels was from the Hebrew language, going against the thought of Augustine, who believed the Greek was inspired. Jerome had a copy of the gospel of Matthew in Hebrew in 390 AD. Eusebius also tells us that Pantaenus, a Christian theologian, around 190 AD, went to India on a missionary journey, and found that one of Jesus' apostles, Bartholomew, (Nathanael) had taken the gospel of Matthew to India written in the Hebrew language. Epiphinius, who was the Bishop of Salamis, Cyprus, (310–403 AD), was a careful student of the scriptures, and also spoke five languages, including Hebrew, believed that Matthew's gospel was originally written in the Hebrew language.

But the primary reason we believe that the gospel of Matthew was written in Hebrew originally, is because of the styles of his writing. There are many Hebrew styles, such as; a) <u>remez</u>, *(hint of the Messiah)* b) <u>gematria</u>, *(numerical value of Hebrew letters)* c) <u>hyperboles</u>, *(extreme illustrations)* d) <u>kalvyhomers</u>, *(comparing the less with the greater)* e) <u>paradoxes</u>, *(seemingly contradictions)* f) <u>word puns</u> *(words that sound similar with different meanings)* and g) <u>string of pearls</u> *(stringing a part of a verse with another verse)*. Matthew was writing to Hebrew-speaking Jews in the first century. In the Greek thought, there are *prophecies* and *fulfillment*, but only from the philosophical viewpoint. In the Hebrew thought, there are *prophecies* and *fulfillment*, then there are certain *patterns* that result in a godly way of living. There is the *contextual* truth, and then there may be a *hidden message* within that context that pertains to the coming Messiah. Many times God had spoken through the prophets a deeper meaning than the prophets understood at the time.

There are four major ways of interpreting the sacred scriptures:

1) *P'Shat*—The literal context of the passage, the true meaning.

2) *Remez*—A hint of something deeper, like a hint of the coming Messiah woven within a P'Shat.

3) *Midrash*—Finding a meaning in the passage that is allegorical, something different than the true meaning but is still applicable.

4) *Sod*—a secret, hidden meaning, like a numerical value of a combination of letters in a certain word.

The sacred scriptures were written by forty authors over a period of two thousand years, and yet it is one integrated design by God. The truths had to originate outside the dimension of time, from an eternal Being. The scriptures fit together like a beautiful piece of woven tapestry. The gospels stand at the center of the Bible and depict our Savior in four different ways:

1) MATTHEW—KING—*WHAT HE SAID*
2) MARK—SERVANT—*WHAT HE DID*
3) LUKE—MAN—*WHAT HE FELT*
4) JOHN—GOD—*WHO HE WAS*

Matthew was a former tax collector, so he would have been an excellent accountant. He would have written his gospel on a scroll; the codex, notebook style would not come along until later in the first century, used by the apostle Paul (**2 Timothy 4:13**).

Matthew's gospel records the Sermon on the Mount in chapters 5, 6, and 7, containing 111 verses; and 53 verses are used in the kingdom parables in **Matthew 13**. Matthew also mentions several instances of money in his gospel, showing his interest in finances.

The date of Matthew's gospel is unknown, but is believed now to have been the first gospel written. Some scholars believe it was written not long after Jesus ascended back to heaven, possibly in the late 30s.

Schofield's Bible dates it at 37 AD. It has been the most influential gospel in the history of the church, and that is why it was placed as the first book of the New Testament in the canon of scripture. Ignatius, (107 AD), quotes Matthew's gospel, as does Polycarp (156 AD), and Justin Martyr (165 AD).

The emphasis on Jesus being Israel's Messiah, the bridge between the Old and New Testaments, and the fulfillment of the promises that God made to Abraham, that salvation would not only come to Israel, but to the rest of the world as well, proves that God keeps His promises. As we embark on this spiritual journey through Matthew's gospel, I can't help but to be reminded of the similarities of the dark days of the first century and the dark days in which we live today. Matthew did not allow this to discourage him from writing his gospel, and we must not allow the unbelief of our day to discourage us from writing this commentary and applying these truths to our own lives. Just as the Messiah was God in the flesh, Who lived and walked among us, experiencing all of the woes and struggles that we face, He won the victory. Jesus the Christ proved that through His power we too can have the victory. As we strive to be filled with His Spirit, we can walk in His footsteps. My prayer is that these truths will find a resting place in our hearts and will be applied to our daily lives. The gospel of Jesus the Christ is truth accompanied by power!

Chapter One

Matthew starts his gospel with the genealogy of the Messiah, which is boring to the average reader but very important if you were a Jew in the first century expecting the Messiah to come through the lineage and the house of David. What is so condescending is the fact that the God of the universe humbled Himself to be born in the flesh and to even *have* a genealogy. Thus proving how much He desired to let us know how much He loved us and wanted to be with us.

Following the Babylonian captivity, the Jewish community was very keen on tracing genealogical records to ensure family purity. Matthew, being a Jew himself, knew that any Jew, who desired to trust in Jesus of Nazareth as the long-awaited Messiah, would want to know about His ancestry first.

I don't know about you, but when I research the background on some of my relatives I find some rather rough subjects. It amazes people sometimes to find that some of their ancestors were pirates, cut throats, and thieves. The same was in the genealogy of the Messiah; we find some of the best and some of the worst in humanity. We need to carefully read this first chapter and see how God's grace played such a role in bringing the Messiah into the world.

Matthew 1:1—*"The book of the generation of Jesus Christ, the son of David, the son of Abraham."*

In the book of Genesis, we find the story of creation and God's covenant relations with Israel. Matthew is using the pattern from **Genesis 5:1**: *"This is the book of the generations of Adam."* Using this pattern would have been familiar to any Jewish person of his day, and it would have linked Jesus the Messiah to the fulfillment of the covenants that God made to Abraham and to David, and presented Him as man's representative as Adam was also man's representative.

The combination of the words *Jesus Christ* is a transliteration of the Greek words *Iesous Christos,* but the original Hebrew would have been, *Yeshua Ha Mashiach.* The word *Yeshua* comes from the word *Yehoshua,* and it means "Yahweh saves." The words *Ha Mashiach* mean "the anointed." Thus, *Yeshua* was His name and *Messiah* was His title.

Matthew tells us in the first verse of his gospel that Jesus was the "Son of David." He emphasizes this many times throughout his gospel, because the term, *Son of David* was considered a Messianic title in the early first century. It was developed, no doubt, from passages such as, **Isaiah 11:1, 10**, *"a root of Jesse,"* and a *"Branch unto David,"* from **Jeremiah 23:5, 33:15, Zechariah 3:8, 6:12**.

God promised David in **2 Samuel 7:12–16**, that one of his descendants would be seated upon the throne of Israel forever. Even the scribes and Pharisees believed this truth. David was anointed by Samuel in **1 Samuel 16:13**, and Jesus was the Anointed One of God that would fulfill the Davidic Covenant.

But Matthew goes on to say that Jesus is the *"son of Abraham."* This was not a Messianic title, but rather expressed the Jewishness of Jesus. God promised Abraham that his seed would bless the nations, so the Savior must be a true Israelite. This seed was none other than Christ Himself, in **Galatians 3:16**. When God changed Avram's name to *Avraham*, this meant that he would be the father of many nations (**Genesis 17:5**). But it also showed that Yahweh had breathed on Avram and placed the "H" sound in his name. This is such an important theme in the scriptures, that Paul uses it in **Romans 4:1–25**, and **Galatians 3:6–29**, showing that many Gentiles would be *"children of Abraham"* by faith. Jesus even said that, *"many shall come* *from the east and west, and sit down with Abraham, Isaac, and Jacob"* (**Matthew 8:11**), by which He is apparently speaking about Gentiles. Likewise, John the Baptist said, *"God is able of these stones to raise up children to Abraham"* (**Matthew 3:9**).

So when Matthew uses the dual, "son of David, son of Abraham," he is referring to Jesus and the True King of Israel, and He will bring salvation to the nations as well. The opening verse of Matthew's gospel is setting the stage for the entire gospel.

Matthew 1:2–11—*"Abraham begat Isaac; and Isaac begat Jacob; and Jacob begat Judas and his brethren; And Judas begat Phares and Zara of Thamar; and Phares begat Esrom; and Esrom begat Aram; And Aram begat Aminadab; and Aminadab begat Naason; and Naason begat Salmon; And Salmon begat Booz of Rachab; and Booz begat Obed of Ruth; and Obed begat Jesse; And Jesse begat David the king; and David the king begat Solomon of her that had been the wife of Urias; And Solomon begat Roboam; and Roboam begat Abia; and Abia begat Asa; And Asa begat Josaphat; and Josaphat begat Joram; and Joram begat Ozias; And Ozias begat Joatham; and Joatham begat Achaz; and Achaz begat Ezekias; And Ezekias begat Manasses; and Manasses begat Amon; and Amon begat Josias; And Josias begat Jechonias and his brethren, about the time they were carried away to Babylon;"*

The fact that Matthew gives a *descending* genealogy is also proof of the original Hebrew writing. Luke gives an *ascending* genealogy, which was common in Greco-Roman genealogies.

1) <u>There is much that can be said about the importance</u> that many of these names played in the line of the Messiah. For example: **Abraham** is the father of the Jewish people (**Genesis 12**). **Isaac** is a perfect type of the Messiah (**Genesis 22**). The Messiah came through the tribe of **Judah (Hebrews 7:14).**

Phares means, "to split," or "make a breach," which is connected to **Micah 2:13**, pointing to the coming Messiah. **Naason** was believed to have been the first one to enter into the Red Sea at the Exodus, when all others were afraid. **Booz** is considered one of the godliest men in the history of Israel by being the kinsman redeemer (**Ruth 4**). David is the greatest king in Israel's history, known as the "son of Jesse." (**1 Samuel 16; Isaiah 11:1, 10**) **Josaphat,** (**1 Kings 22**) **Joatham,** (**2 Kings 15:32–38; 2 Chronicles 27**) **Ezekias,** (Hezekiah), (**2 Kings 18–20; 1 Chronicles 29–32; Isaiah 36–39**) and **Josiah** (**2 Kings 21–23**) were all good kings in the history of Israel.

2) <u>*There is much that can be said about the wickedness*</u> of many of these names in the history of Israel. For example: **Judah** committed incest with **Tamar (Genesis 38). David** committed adultery and murder. (**2 Samuel 11–12**) **Solomon's** heart was turned away from the Lord by his many strange, pagan wives (**1 Kings 11:1–8**). **Roboam** was known as a wicked king, having adopted pagan practices (**1 Kings 14:21–24; 2 Chronicles 12:13–14**). **Joram** was an evil king (**2 Kings 8:16–24**). **Achaz** was considered to be an apostate (**2 Kings 16, 2; Chronicles 28**). **Manasses** was the most wicked of the kings of Judah (**2 Kings 21:1–18, 2; Chronicles 33:1–9**). There was a curse placed on **Jechonias** and his seed for his youthful wickedness (**Jeremiah 22:30**). And to add more sadness to the Messianic line: *"they were carried away to Babylon,"* because of their idolatry. The wickedness in the Messianic line and the curse that was placed on Jechonias necessitated a virgin birth.

3) <u>*There is much that can be said about the women*</u> who are mentioned in Matthew's genealogy. Women were not commonly listed in Jewish genealogies. For example: **Thamar** played the harlot to her father-in-law, Judah (**Genesis 38**). **Rachab** was a Canaanite (**Joshua 2, 6; Matthew 1:5; Hebrews 11:31; James 2:25**). **Rachab** means "broad" or "large."

Compare this with **Exodus 3:8**. She was considered to be one of the most beautiful women in the world, although she used it in a seductive way. **Ruth**, a Moabite, (**Ruth 1**), was part of one of the most beautiful stories in the Old Testament of mercy and grace. For her to be listed in the genealogy of the Messiah is remarkable, because the Torah prohibited the descendants of Moab from entering the assembly of the Lord for ten generations. (**Read Genesis 19:36–37**; **Deuteronomy 23:3**) "The wife of Urias," better known as *Bat-sheva*, was a Hittite, who was part of the adulterous affair with King David, but also was the mother of Solomon (**2 Samuel 11–12**).

By including these women, Matthew was emphasizing that not only did they play a role in the line of the Messiah, but it also showed that God was reversing the gender marginalization of women that was prominent in Judaism. We can see this also with the story of the Samaritan woman in **John 4**, and the women from Galilee in **Luke 8:1–3**.

Matthew 1:12–16—*"And after they were brought to Babylon, Jeconias begat Salathiel; and Salathiel begat Zorobabel; And Zorobabel begat Abiud; and Abiud begat Eliakim; and Eliakim begat Azor; and Azor begat Sadoc; and Sadoc begat Achim; and Achim begat Eliud; And Eliud begat Eleazar; and Eleazar begat Matthan; and Matthan begat Jacob; And Jacob begat Joseph the husband of Mary, of whom was born Jesus, who is called Christ."*

In this list of seemingly unimportant names, God is showing us that the Messiah came into the world from everyday people and that God worked through seemingly unimportant people to bring the Messiah into the world. He did not *"come to call the righteous but sinners to repentance."* For the most part, there is little record of most of these names except here in Matthew's gospel. Zorobabel, or Zerubbabel, was a descendant of David, and Zechariah speaks about Zerubbabel as one through whom the Lord would rebuild the temple and re-establish the nation (**Zechariah 4:6–10**).

Sadoc, or Zadok, was a priest in the court of David (**2 Samuel 8:17**). Most of these names were common in the Old Testament and are still widely used today within Judaism. In this list of names, Matthew is bringing us to Yeshua, the Messiah.

I find **verse 16** to be very significant, because Joseph would be only a bystander if it were not for Matthew's account. The name *Yoseph* means, "he adds." Joseph was one of the most popular names in the first century, and still is today. There is a clear change in the wording here, from "X begat Y," to ***"of whom was born Jesus."*** Matthew was showing that the Messiah was "virgin born," and not born into the world as the others listed in the genealogy. The virgin birth of Christ was accepted by the Jewish believers in the first century, but was a very hard apologetic for the unbelieving Jew, so the verbal usage in this verse changed. Matthew also changes the wording to show that the Holy Spirit brought Jesus into the world through a woman, without the need of a human father. Even though one of the first century names of Jesus was, *Yeshua ben Yoseph*, Joseph was not Jesus' real father, but Joseph was viewed as Jesus' *legal* father.

The most important part of the verse is: ***"who is called Christ,"*** which comes from the Greek word, *Christos*, meaning, "to anoint." The Hebrew original would have been *Mashiach*, which means, "one who is anointed." Matthew is simply stating that the One that came through the virgin womb of Mary, was the long-awaited Messiah of Israel. Praise God! The *"seed of the serpent"* could not prevent the *"Seed of the woman"* from coming into the world (**Genesis 3:15**).

Matthew 1:17— *"So all the generations from Abraham to David are fourteen generations; and from David until the carrying away into Babylon are fourteen generations; and from the carrying away into Babylon unto Christ are fourteen generations."*

Matthew deliberately skips some generations in Jesus' family tree so that the structure can be made for **three** sets of fourteen. This is a subtle reference to King David. The Jewish practice of counting the numerical value for letters is called, *gematria*. When one writes David, just using the consonants, you have, **d v d = 4+6+4 = 14**. So there is an encoded theological meaning, which also helps with memorization. The Messiah had to be the *"Son of David."*

Matthew 1:18—*"Now the birth of Jesus Christ was on this wise: When as his mother Mary was espoused to Joseph, before they came together, she was found with child of the Holy Ghost."*

With the genealogy having been concluded, Matthew goes on to describe in brief the circumstances that brought Jesus into the world. Notice the reverse order from **verse 16**, Joseph, Mary, and Jesus, here in **verse 18**, it is, Jesus, Mary, and Joseph. The verbal usage in **verse 16** is now being explained. Mary is called, "the mother of Jesus," but Joseph is never called the father of Jesus. Matthew's intent is to show the first-century Jewish readers that Yeshua was the divine "Son of Man," whose Father is the God of Israel.

The term, **"espoused to Joseph before they came together"** was a betrothal period, which lasted about one year before a couple was officially married. Even though they were not married officially, there were clear legal ramifications that existed between the couple (**Deuteronomy 20:7, 28:30; Judges 14:15, 15:1; 2 Samuel 3:14**). If the future husband died during this betrothal period, the woman was considered a widow. And the betrothal could only be dissolved by divorce. If something happened that the man left during the betrothal period, or that the betrothal was dissolved, (unless the woman was guilty of bad conduct) a compensation was required, probably the retaining of the bride price that was paid at betrothal. **"Before they came together,"** Joseph and Mary had not had sexual relations, and Mary would have resided in the home of her father. Once again, we see the importance of the virgin birth; Mary was not carrying Joseph's child.

"She was found with child by the Holy Ghost," tells us that the readers in the first century, and us today, were given insight that even Joseph did not have at the time. Joseph will learn this in time that the child that Mary is carrying is a work of the blessed *Ruach Ha Qodesh*, or the Holy Spirit. In Jewish thinking, this also parallels the creation story in **Genesis 1**, where the power of the Holy Spirit is at work. The virgin birth of the Messiah was anticipated by the giving of circumcision as the sign of the Abrahamic covenant, and the supernatural birth of Isaac (**Genesis 21**).

It was also believed that the Holy Spirit was at work when the midwives did not kill the male children down in the land of Egypt, as Pharaoh ordered them to do (**Exodus 1**). The coming of the Messiah was the fulfillment and the anticipation of the ages. What took place within the womb of the little Virgin Mary would forever change the course of human history.

Matthew 1:19—*"Then Joseph her husband, being a just man, and not willing to make her a public example, was minded to put her away privily."*

The betrothal period was so binding that Joseph was called, ***"her husband." "Being a just man, and not willing to make her a public example, was minded to put her away privily."*** Joseph was a keeper of the Law of Moses, and he knew that the pregnancy of Mary during their betrothal period called for a divorce, (**Deuteronomy 24:1**) so he wanted to keep the law by divorcing Mary, but he also did not want to bring public shame to her. Thus Joseph was "just" in two ways. This is overlooked many times in our studies of the Christmas story. So he decided to divorce her secretly, because Mary could have been stoned. Satan would have loved to have had Mary stoned. Matthew is telling us the significance of a ***"just man"*** like Joseph was during the birth of the Messiah.

Matthew 1:20— *"But while he thought on these things, behold, the angel of the Lord appeared unto him in a dream, saying, Joseph, thou son of David, fear not to take thee Mary thy wife: for that which is conceived in her is of the Holy Ghost."*

The characteristic of a godly man is that he carefully considers things before he acts, and this is what Joseph did. He did not rush to judgment. ***"The angel of the Lord appeared unto him in a dream."*** This is the first of four dreams that were given to Joseph. In each case the dream is related to Jesus, providing supernatural divine guidance. It does not give the name of the angel here, but it could have been Gabriel, since he was the one who spoke to Daniel about the time when the Messiah was to come into the world in **Daniel 9:21–25**, and Gabriel was the angel who came to the mother Mary in **Luke 1:26.**

"Joseph, thou son of David," reinforces the fact that Joseph is legally the earthly father of Yeshua, and is from the house of David. When the religious leaders would later try to condemn Jesus within the context of His healing ministry, many of the common people knew that Jesus came from the house of David (**Matthew 12:23**).

So this is why the Holy Spirit, through Matthew, is constantly stating that even the earthly family of Jesus came from the lineage of David.

"Fear not <u>to take</u> *unto* ***thee Mary thy wife,"*** Many times in the Old Testament and in the life and ministry of Christ, the words "do not fear" are used. The messenger was assuring Joseph that is was okay to go ahead and <u>to take</u> Mary back to his home as the final step of the marriage process.

"For that which is conceived in her is of the Holy Ghost." Here is the ultimate truth; Mary is pregnant, not as the result of fornication, but by the direct act of God. The Holy ***"Ghost,"*** which comes from the old English translation, is the same as the Holy "Spirit." And not only is the blessed Holy Spirit used here as the agency of God, but is used as a person distinct from the Father and the Son.

Matthew 1:21—*"And she shall bring forth a son, and thou shalt call his name JESUS: for he shall save his people from their sins."*

Notice the gender would be a "son," and the fact that the angel is telling Joseph to name the male child confirms that Joseph is to accept Him as his own. The English name, "JESUS" comes from the Greek, *IESOUS*, but neither one of these names have a definitive meaning. The Hebrew word, *YEHOSHUA, (or Yeshua),* is the only name that means, "salvation." Here it is clear that the Hebrew is superior. The Messiah is coming to ***"save his people from their sins,"*** Israel. This correlates with the writings of the prophets and the gospel of Matthew, that salvation is coming to God's chosen people. But the prophets also taught that salvation would come to the Gentiles (**Genesis 49:10; Deuteronomy 32:43; Isaiah 42:4, 56:3–7; Zechariah 8:23**).

Sin has to be dealt with. Sin is not relative; there is a judgment coming. God is HOLY, HOLY, HOLY, (**Isaiah 6:3**), and the only remedy is salvation through the sinless Messiah, *Yeshua Ha Mashiach*, the Lord Jesus Christ.

Matthew 1:22–23—*"Now all this was done, that it might be fulfilled which was spoken of the Lord by the prophet, saying, Behold, a virgin shall be with child, and shall bring forth a son, and they shall call his name Emmanuel, which being interpreted is, God with us."*

Matthew emphasizes the overarching divine providence by which all of these events were set into place concerning the birth of the Messiah. The scripture referred to is **Isaiah 7:14** ***"That it might be fulfilled which was spoken by the Lord by the prophet."*** Notice, it was the Lord doing the speaking through the prophet. So how does **Isaiah 7:14** refer to the Messiah? This is another example of a *remez*, a hint of the coming Messiah hidden within the Old Testament. In the context, Isaiah is saying that in the dark days of Israel's history in the eighth-century BC, the birth of their own children was to remind them that God was still with them, and that He would secure their deliverance from their enemies. But within the text is the hope of the coming Messiah in the future that ultimately delivers Israel. True peace would eventually come through the coming Redeemer.

"Behold, a virgin shall be with child." There are two words in the Hebrew for virgin. The word *almah*, which occurs in **Isaiah 7:14**, means "maiden, young girl" and never refers to a married woman. The other word, *betulah*, can mean a "virgin," but also can mean "old widow." The Hebrew word used is *almah*, which almost without exception specifies an unmarried woman who is a virgin.

"They shall call his name Emmanuel, which being interpreted is, God with us." The name given to the Redeemer is, Immanuel, in **Isaiah 7:14**, meaning "God (is) with us." Throughout the Old Testament, the presence of God with His people assures them of His protection and salvation (**Genesis 26:24; Deuteronomy 31:8; 1 Chronicles 28:20; 2 Chronicles 20:17; Isaiah 41:10, 43:5; Jeremiah 46:28**). In the sacred name of God, "I Am" in **Exodus 3:14**, *"Eheyeh,"* "I will be," the idea of God's presence is connected (**Exodus 3:12, 4:12, 4:15**). So the name of the Messiah will bear the essence of God's sacred name, *God with us*. His earthly name, *Yeshua*, would describe "what He does," while, *Immanuel* specifies "who He is." The very presence of The Lord God Almighty will be with His people. WOW!

Matthew added the interpretation of the name maybe because many of the Jewish readers were Hellenized into the Greek culture and language. Matthew is intent on making sure that his readers understand the meaning of the word *Immanuel*, and where it came from.

Matthew 1:24–25— *"Then Joseph being raised from the sleep did as the angel of the Lord had bidden him, and took unto him his wife: and knew her not till she had brought forth her firstborn son: and he called his name JESUS."*

Matthew concludes the birth narrative with a "pattern of obedience" that is mentioned throughout the Old Testament, particularly in the book of Exodus, where we find statements like: *"just as the Lord had commanded Moses."* Joseph is seen as a righteous man, who obeys the commandments of God. **"And took unto him his wife: and knew her not till she had brought forth her firstborn son."** Normally, the marriage was consummated through physical union the night of the wedding, but here we find that Joseph did not have sexual relations with Mary until <u>after</u> the birth of Jesus. The teaching of the Catholic Church has been for centuries that Mary remained a virgin after the birth of Jesus, but it is clear in the scriptures that she and Joseph did have other children (**Matthew 12:46, 13:55–56; John 7:5**). It has been argued that the word for *brothers* can also mean cousins, but in **Matthew 13:56,** the word for *sisters* can only refer to sisters, not cousins. Also, the Bible would have avoided the term *firstborn* if Mary had remained a virgin.

"And he called his name JESUS." This reiterates **verse 21**, with the second person, "you" changed to the third person, "he." Once again, the obedience of Joseph is highlighted. This also emphasizes that all of the promises of the first coming of the Messiah found their fulfillment in the Person of Yeshua.

Chapter Two

Matthew 2:1–2—*"Now when Jesus was born in Bethlehem of Judaea in the days of Herod the king, behold, there came wise men from the east to Jerusalem, Saying, where is he that is born King of the Jews? For we have seen his star in the east, and are come to worship him."*

After focusing on "Who" the Messiah was in chapter one, showing His connection to the royal line of David, Matthew now describes how the true King Messiah would be received. Matthew's gospel does not record the lowly shepherds that are recorded in **Luke 2**. But I would like to mention that a shepherd was considered by the religious leaders to be a very unclean person in society. They were constantly around sheep and goat dung, and touching dead things, so they were not allowed to worship in the temple or the synagogues. It is very important that we realize that God did not come to the so-called religious people of the day when the birth of the Messiah was announced. God sees the heart, and He saw the hearts of the lowly shepherds more pure than the priests in the temple. So in the midst of talking about Herod the king, and the wise men, let us not forget that the shepherds were the very first visitors to the Christ child.

"*Now when Jesus was born in Bethlehem of Judaea."* It helps to understand that the idea of *BC*, (before Christ) and *AD*, (Anno Domini, in the year of our Lord), originated with the sixth-century, Scythian monk named Dionysius Exiguus. He made a mistake in the calendar, and that is why we have Jesus being born in a BC date. The best date for the birth that fits the biblical text with Jewish writings and historians is sometime in September, in 2 BC. Many commentaries and study Bibles place the birth of Jesus in 4–5 BC, but that was based on a natural phenomenon in the stars that occurred, trying to fit that into the text. But the birth of Christ was supernatural. It is documented that Jesus of Nazareth was born twenty-eight years after the death of Cleopatra, who committed suicide in 30 BC. It is also documented that Herod the Great died fifteen years prior to Augustus Caesar, who died in August of 14 AD, placing Herod's death in 1 BC. This fits the biblical text of Jesus being born when Herod the Great was king. The gospel of **Luke 3:1**, says John the Baptist started his ministry in the fifteenth year of the reign of Tiberias Caesar, (began to reign on the 19th of August, 14 AD). This places John's ministry starting in approximately 28 AD. In **Luke 3:23**, it states that Jesus was about thirty years old at His baptism. When one does the arithmetic, this places the birth of Jesus also around 2 BC.

Where was the Messiah born? In Bethlehem of Judaea, located about five or six miles south of Jerusalem. This continues to link the Messiah with the lineage of David (**Luke 2:4; John 7:42**). David lived in Bethlehem and was anointed king of Israel there (**1 Samuel 16:1–13**). Bethlehem was also the place where Rachel was buried, (**Genesis 35:19**), as well as the city in which the story of Ruth is set (**Ruth 1:19**).

Bethlehem in Judaea separates the southern Bethlehem from the northern Bethlehem, which was located seven miles northwest of Nazareth.

The word *Beit-Lechem* means "house of bread." There is a beautiful connection here with what Jesus proclaimed in **John 6:48**, when he said, *"I am that bread of Life."*

"In the days of Herod the king." Who is Herod? Which Herod is he? He was Herod the Great. In the gospels we have four Herods:

1) Herod the Great—(37–1 BC) **Matthew 2:1**
2) Herod Archelaus—(1 BC–6 AD) **Matthew 2:22**
3) Herod Antipas—(1 BC–39 AD) **Matthew 14:1, Luke 3:1**
4) Herod Philip—(1 BC–34 AD) **Luke 3:1**

Herod the Great, **(37–1 BC)**, was a puppet king, placed in Israel by Rome. He was one of the most wicked kings who ever lived. He would not only kill one of his wives, (Miramne I) but two of his own sons, (Alexander and Aristobulus). Anyone or anything that threatened his throne was in danger of being killed. He was paranoid and lived in constant fear that he was going to lose his position. He built fortresses and palaces all over the land of Israel, at Caesarea, (on the Mediterranean Sea coast) Sebaste, (in Samaria) Herodium, (in Bethlehem) Masada, (by the Dead Sea), Machaerus, Jericho, as well as, built the second temple in Jerusalem. One reason for building all of these fortresses was because he was worried about being deposed and he wanted a place of safety to retreat to. The reason he built the temple in Jerusalem was because after killing many of the Jewish religious leaders he asked a rabbi how to receive forgiveness, and the rabbi told him to rebuild the temple.

Herod the Great died from a horrible, venereal disease in Jericho, and was buried in his Herodium palace in Bethlehem. His tomb was discovered inside the ruins of the Herodium in May 2007, by Professor Ehud Netzer, of the university's Institute of Archaeology, after thirty-five years of research.

"There came wise men from the east to Jerusalem." Most all Hebrew scholars agree that these wise men were Gentiles. Matthew is telling us that Gentiles were coming to worship the Messiah, even at His birth. They were called *magi*, where we get the word "magistrate." The Hebrew word for magician is *chartome*, meaning "a horoscopist." They were

astrologers and men who interpreted dreams. They were *"from the east,"* (Gentiles) from either Arabia, Babylon, or Persia. But they were more than typical astrologers; they were *wise sages*, and as they studied the universe, God showed them His glory (**Psalm 19:1–3, 147:4; Job 38:32**). *Mazzaroth* refers to the twelve constellations of the stars around the sun. They read the stars and knew that a King was born in Israel, not some other country, but Israel. There is a strong Jewish tradition that the wise men came from Babylon and that they would have known of the time of the coming Messiah because of the writings of the prophet Daniel. Daniel was made *"chief governor of all of the wise men,"* 600 years before the Messiah came (**Daniel 2:48**). The Lord revealed to Daniel that the Messiah would come 483 years after the decree was signed to rebuild Jerusalem (**Daniel 9:25**). They may have traveled approximately 1000 miles from the east to Jerusalem, and it would have taken weeks or even months. We do not know how many wise men came to Jerusalem, but it probably would have been more than three, possibly a caravan of ten or more.

Today, there is a "Shrine of the Kings," inside the Cologne Cathedral in Germany. It supposedly contains the bones and clothes of the wise men, dating back to the early fourth century. And even though we may have reservations about the authenticity of these relics, the influence of the wise men is still remembered.

"Saying, where is he that is born King of the Jews?" The titles, "King of the Jews" and "Son of David" were synonymous with the Messiah of Israel! Jesus was not going to *be* the king, He was *born* King! One of His earthly names was, *Yeshua Ha Melech*, "Jesus the King." Try to imagine how this must have disturbed King Herod, when the wise men asked where is *the* king? And to make matters even worse, Persia had invaded Israel in 40 BC, and Herod fled to places like Masada for safety. So the fact that these wise men were from Persia must have reminded Herod of the battle that had taken place just a few years earlier.

"For we have seen his star in the east, and are come to worship him." Most all Hebrew scholars connect *"his star,"* with **Numbers 24:17, *"a Star shall come forth out of Jacob,"*** even though Matthew does not refer to it here. This was a supernatural star, not just a conjunction of the planets like some have stated. The star was a visible manifestation of the glory of God, the *Shekinah*, which followed the children of Israel in the wilderness (**Exodus 13:21–22**). The Almighty chose to give these seeking wise men this supernatural sign, and it was so overwhelming that they traveled across the desert to not only follow the star, but to worship the Keeper of the stars. It's also worth mentioning that they came from the "east," the same direction where the Messiah would later come into Jerusalem, and will come back the second time. Ezekiel saw the glory of God coming back to Jerusalem from the east (**Ezekiel 43:2; Zechariah 14:4**).

The Hebrew word for worship, *shachah*, means, "to prostrate, or bow down." Matthew uses the same word twelve times (**Matthew 2:8, 11, 4:9–10, 8:2, 9:18, 14:33, 15:25, 18:26, 20:20, 28:9, 17**).

Matthew 2:3–6—*"When Herod the king had heard these things, he was troubled, and all Jerusalem with him. And when he had gathered all the chief priests and scribes of the people together, he demanded of them where Christ should be born. And they said unto him, In Bethlehem of Judaea: for thus it is written by the prophet, And thou Bethlehem, in the land of Juda, art not the least among the princes of Juda: for out of thee shall come a Governor, that shall rule my people."*

The fact that foreigners had come from so far to worship this King, suggested the undercurrent of revolt, and even the Jewish leaders were seriously troubled with Herod. What a sad state Jerusalem must have been, to be troubled over the birth of the Savior? What is even worse, the religious leaders knew the scriptures where the Messiah was to be born,

Micah 5:2, and still did not recognize the time of their visitation. How could this be? It is because the scribes, who copied down the scriptures, were superimposing their own traditions on the same level as the sacred text. The chief priests were puppets, worried about losing their positions. The rabbi's interpretations were held in such high esteem that they missed the Messiah when He came. How dangerous tradition and religion can be. There have been many false messiahs in Israel's history, and not a one of them were born in Bethlehem.

Notice the changes in the wording of **Micah 5:2**. Instead of saying, *Bethlehem Ephratah*, the religious leaders call it *Bethlehem in Juda*, possibly recognizing Herod's domain. They also do not mention how insignificant Bethlehem really is, like the prophecy in Micah states, but instead they say, **"art not the least among the princes of Juda."** They also seem to downplay the *"ruler in Israel, whose goings forth have been from everlasting,"* to simply, *"shall rule my people Israel."* What a tragedy! To know the geography, and to know theology, but to not know Him!

Matthew 2:7–8—*"Then Herod, when he had privily called the wise men, enquired of them diligently what time the star appeared. And he sent them to Bethlehem, and said, Go and search diligently for the young child; and when ye have found him, bring me word again, that I may come and worship him also."*

Herod has now put together two pieces of information, one from the wise men, that a star appeared, and another from the religious leaders, that the prophets had predicted a ruler to come forth from Bethlehem. But now Herod wants to know when the exact time the star appeared. So he *secretly* calls for the wise men. The initial appearance of the star occurred sometime earlier, but we do not know exactly how long. As we will see a little later, Herod cruelly chose an excessively wide margin of time to assure that the Child was no longer a threat. With the intent to destroy, Herod pretends to worship. The wise men may not have known the wicked heart of Herod, but they would not see him again.

Matthew 2:9–10—*"When they had heard the king, they departed; and lo, the star, which they saw in the east, went before them, till it came and stood over where the young child was. When they saw the star, they rejoiced with exceeding great joy."*

Notice the star seems to appear, disappear, and reappear, once again proving that this was not a natural star; it was the Sovereign Lord giving them His glory when He chose to do so. Now the glory was given to guide them to the location of the Christ Child. This is indicated by the word "lo," or behold. It's interesting that the shepherds also saw God's glory (**Luke 2:9**).

"When they saw the star" This was a confirmation to the wise men about the star they had seen originally. Think about traveling a thousand miles across the desert, following a star, and then the star disappears. Have we lost our way? Are we at the right place? Yes, the star reappeared, and they rejoiced with *"exceeding great joy."* I love the wording here, *"exceeding great joy,"* because this is what the Hebrew word for joy, *simchah*, actually means. Once again, notice the contrast; religious leaders in Jerusalem were troubled at the birth of the Messiah, and Gentiles who had traveled from afar were rejoicing. The prophets were right! Nations would come to the Light of Israel (**Isaiah 42:6, 49:6, 60:3**).

Matthew 2:11—*"And when they were come into the house, they saw the young child with Mary his mother, and fell down, and worshipped him: and when they had opened their treasures, they presented unto him gifts; gold, and frankincense, and myrrh."*

The fact that they came ***"into the house"*** tells us that Joseph and Mary had taken up residence in Bethlehem. The houses were built in rocky, cavernous areas, and the lower floor would contain caves and grottos where the animals would sleep. Our Savior would have been born in a cave, underneath a house.[1] Now, the *"young child"* had moved into a dwelling, possibly a relative of Joseph.

"They fell down and worshipped him." This further illustrates the Hebrew meaning for worship, "falling prostrate on your knees." They did not worship the mother Mary, but "Him" the Christ. The official worship of Mary started with the Ecumenical Council of Ephesus, in 431 AD. Even though Mary was no doubt probably the godliest woman on the planet during the time of Jesus, she is not to be worshipped. She had to have a Savior as well (**Luke 1:47**).

"When they had opened their treasures, they presented unto him gifts; gold, frankincense, and myrrh." All of these gifts were very expensive, and were reserved for royalty. The wise men may have purchased them along their journeys, because the Nabataeans were noted for their expensive products, southeast of the Dead Sea. Many have tried to find an

---

[1] Underneath the Church of Nativity in Bethlehem, (first built by Helena in 325 AD) lies a series of caves, and one of them is believed to be the place where Jesus was born. I remember the very first time I was there, how I couldn't stop weeping, just to think that the God of the universe would humble Himself to be born in such a lowly place, and why? So sinful people like you and I could touch Him by faith! One of my favorite old Christmas songs was written by Phillip Brooks, a pastor from Philadelphia, in 1868, while he was overlooking the shepherd fields in Bethlehem:

> **O little town of Bethlehem, how still we see thee lie.**
> **Above thy deep and dreamless sleep, The silent stars go by.**
> **Yet in thy dark streets shineth the Everlasting Light.**
> **The hopes and fears of all the years are met in thee tonight.**

extensive meaning of the gifts. It is true that gold could refer to the Lord's "kingship," frankincense is indicative of His, "divinity," and myrrh as a symbol of His "sacrificial death." The best place to get a deeper meaning is the Old Testament, where the prophets foresaw a time when the nations would come and present gifts to the Lord (**Isaiah 18:7, 60:5–6; Psalm 72:9–11**). It is also believed that the costly gifts helped to fund the journey of the holy family into Egypt.

Matthew 2:12—*"And being warned of God in a dream that they should not return to Herod, they departed into their own country another way."*[2]

What a surprise to many of the Jewish readers in the first century that foreigners would receive a divine revelation in concert with the appearance of the Jewish Messiah. The wise men found out through a God-given dream, that King Herod had no intentions of truly worshiping the Messiah. It has been rightly stated that, "once someone has seen the Christ, they travel a different way."

Matthew 2:13–15—*"And when they were departed, behold, the angel of the Lord appeareth to Joseph in a dream, saying, Arise, and*

---

[2] Persia once again invaded the Holy Land in the fifth century AD. They were commanded to tear down the church of nativity that was built by Helena, Constantine's mother, in 325 AD, over the place where Christ was born. When the Persians saw a painting on the inside of the church depicting the wise men being dressed in Persian attire, they changed their minds. Thus, one of the oldest churches in the world still stands in Bethlehem over the cave where the Savior of the world was born.

take the young child and his mother, and flee to Egypt, and be thou there until I bring thee word: for Herod will seek the young child to destroy him. When he arose, he took the young child and his mother by night, and departed into Egypt. And was there until the death of Herod: that it might be fulfilled which was spoken of the Lord by the prophet, saying, Out of Egypt have I called my son."

It's interesting to me that the holy family had intentions of living in Bethlehem, where Jesus was born. They took the baby Jesus to the temple in Jerusalem in **Luke 2:21–24**, to be circumcised and to offer up a sacrifice, forty days after the birth, then they returned back to Bethlehem. If not for the Lord guiding Joseph to go to Egypt, they would have remained in the city of David.

Once again, God is revealing to Joseph in a dream how to protect the Messiah from the powers of darkness. The Lord tells Joseph through the angel to flee into Egypt which was approximately eighty miles from the border.

This passage of scripture is a strange, but a true parallel to the Exodus story. As Pharaoh killed the male children down in the land of Egypt, (**Exodus 1**), Herod killed the male children in Bethlehem. As Moses led the children of Israel out of Egypt, the Messiah came to lead His people out of the slavery of sin. Egypt, in the Old Testament, became a symbol of slavery and trouble (**Genesis 12, 26:2, 37:25, 28; Exodus 1**).

"When he arose, he took the young child and his mother." Notice the obedience of Joseph to act immediately, taking the child and his mother into Egypt at night. Egypt was outside of Herod's jurisdiction, having a Jewish population of over a million people at this time. The Israelites left Egypt also at night (**Exodus 12:29**).

During the period between 320 BC and 198 BC, Israel's geography fell between the wars between Syria and Egypt, and many Jews were established in Egypt. This is also the period of time when the Old

Testament was translated into Greek, called the Septuagint, because of the Hellenized, Greek-speaking Jews (around 285 BC.).

The fulfillment of **Hosea 11:1**, *"Out of Egypt I have called my son,"* is another example of the hidden meanings sometimes in a verse of scripture. It is called a *remez*. It is clear that **Hosea 11:1** is referring to Israel. But as far back as **Exodus 4:22**, Israel is called "God's Son." The Messiah is also referred to as "God's Son" in places like, **Psalm 2:7, 2 Samuel 7:14, Isaiah 9:6,** and **Proverbs 30:4**. The Davidic covenant had a "father/son" language. So Jesus becomes the *greater* Son. Jesus the Messiah is being identified with His people Israel. Matthew is bringing forward the overall Messianic promises of the Hebrew scriptures.

Matthew 2:16—*"Then Herod, when he saw that he was mocked of the wise men, was exceeding wroth, and sent forth, and slew all the children that were in Bethlehem, and in all the coasts thereof, from two years old and under, according to the time which he had diligently enquired of the wise men."*

The word of the angel given to Joseph has come true. Herod, when he realized that the wise men had failed to cooperate with his plan, became outraged and initiates his plan, hoping to destroy the infant King. Only the male children were killed, like during the time of Pharaoh.

Notice that Herod just went ahead and killed the children *"two years old and under,"* trying to make sure that he didn't miss Jesus.[3] This does not necessarily mean that Jesus was two years old; He may have been somewhere between one and two years old.

---

[3] I once asked a biblical historian who lived in Bethlehem, "How many children do you think Herod killed?" His answer was based on the population at that time: "In the neighborhood of seventy." Other sources say between twenty and thirty.

Matthew 2:17–18—*"Then was fulfilled that which was spoken by Jeremy the prophet, saying, In Rama was there a voice heard, lamentation, and weeping, and great mourning, Rachel weeping for her children, and would not be comforted, because they were not."*

The appeal to **Jeremiah 31:15**, once again is a *remez*. Centuries earlier, Nebuchadnezzar's army had gathered the captives from Judah in the town of Ramah, before they were taken to Babylon (**Jeremiah 40:1–2**). Jeremiah depicts Rachel, who is the personification of the mothers of Israel, mourning for her children as they are being carried away. Notice the three strong words: lamentation, weeping, and mourning. Matthew has connected the death of the children in Bethlehem to the situation that occurred hundreds of years earlier. Rachel's tomb is located in Ramah today, just outside of Bethlehem.

But the connection goes even deeper when we look closely at **Jeremiah 31,** because this is the chapter where the *New Covenant* is given (**Jeremiah 31:31–34**). The appearance of the Messiah would bring to fulfillment the New Covenant. There are several parallels between **Jeremiah 31** and **Matthew 1 & 2**.

> **Jeremiah 31: 4, 21**—*O virgin of Israel* = **Matthew 1:23**
> **Jeremiah 31:8**—*Expectant mothers* = **Matthew 1:18**
> **Jeremiah 31:7**—*Save your people* = **Matthew 1:21**
> **Jeremiah 31:17**—*Return to the land* = **Matthew 2:20-21**
> **Jeremiah 31:35**—*The stars to shine by night* = **Matthew 2:2**

Matthew 2:19–21—*"But when Herod was dead, behold, an angel of the Lord appeareth in a dream to Joseph in Egypt, Saying, Arise, and take the young child and his mother, and go into the land of Israel: for they are dead which sought the young child's life. And he arose, and took the young child and his mother, and came into the land of Israel."*

It would have taken a while for the news of the death of wicked Herod to have reached Egypt, but the Lord knew immediately, and sent an angel to tell Joseph to come back into Israel. The world is better off when some people die; they are only a tool of Satan. Anytime Christ is about to do His work, there will always be a Herod around, but Christ will always prevail, thank God! We do not know how long the holy family was in Egypt. One Jewish source, the gospel of Thomas, says one year, but that is only speculation.

Joseph obeyed the word of the Lord, and brought his family back into the **"land of Israel,"** *Eretz-Israel*, not <u>Palestine</u>. *Palestine* was the name given to Israel by the Romans around 135 AD, by the Emperor Hadrian, derived from the name, *Philistines*, trying to blot out the name of *Judaea*. A religious Jew would never call Israel, Palestine.

Matthew 2:22—*"But when he heard that Archelaus did reign in Judaea in room of his father Herod, he was afraid to go thither: notwithstanding, being warned of God in a dream, he turned aside into the parts of Galilee."*

Herod the Great had decreed that his son, Antipas, should be his successor over Judaea, but at his death he changed his mind, and named Archelaus the successor to the throne. Herod Antipas was named the tetrarch of Galilee and Perea, while Herod Philip was named tetrarch over Iturea and Trachonitis. Of the three sons, Philip was the best natured, and the Messiah would use his territory later in his earthly ministry. Archelaus was the worst of the three; he killed 3,000 Pharisees at one time, even though Archelaus was only about nineteen years old at the time. He was hated so much that a Jewish and Samaritan envoy traveled all the way to Rome complaining about his evil schemes. He was deposed to Vienne, in Gaul, in 6 AD, fearing a revolt was on the way. After then, Roman governors, or procurators, were placed in charge of Judaea.

Again, Joseph would have settled with his family in southern Israel, but God would not allow it, and Joseph was sent into northern Israel, *"into the parts of Galilee."* Galilee was not the most loved place in the world to the religious Jews. Galilee had a mixed Jew/Gentile population, and it was where many of the lower class folk lived. Our Lord would have His ministry mostly among the common people of the day.

Before we leave this intriguing, but wonderful part of the early life of our Lord, we can see three important truths:

1) The wise men traveled farther than anyone to see the Messiah. This was a sign that nations would come to Christ from all over the world.

2) The children killed in Bethlehem were the first martyrs for our Lord in the New Testament.

3) The world was a very dark place when the Messiah came the first time, and the world will be a dark place when He returns.

Matthew 2:23—*"And he came and dwelt in a city called Nazareth: that it might be fulfilled which was spoken by the prophets, He shall be called a Nazarene."*

"And he came and dwelt in a city called Nazareth." Nazareth lies about sixty-four miles north of Jerusalem, just north of the Jezreel Valley, and about twenty miles southwest of Capernaum. Less that 500 people lived in Nazareth in the early first century. After the Babylonian captivity, there were some Jews from the Davidic line who settled back in Nazareth. It's very interesting that the Jews who settled there were from the line of David, and gave the settlement a Messianic name. God directed Joseph to not raise Jesus in southern Israel, but in the north, in the town called Nazareth. God governs the affairs of men for His purposes.

Matthew is using a word pun, in describing "Who" the Messiah was and where He lived. **Nazareth**, *natzri;* **Nazarite**, *nazir;* and the **Branch**, *netzer.*

1) Jesus was called in the gospels, *"Jesus of Nazareth"* or, *Yeshua Min Natzri* (**John 1:45, 19:19**). This was part of the humility of the Messiah (**John 1:46; Philippians 2:7**). The Messiah would be despised (**Psalm 22; Isaiah 52–53**).

2) In the book of **Numbers chapter 6**, a *Nazarite,* or, *nazir* was one who was separated "holy" to God. Jesus of Nazareth was called "the Holy One of God" in places like **Mark 1:24**. One of the prophets who was a *Nazarite*, was Samuel. There are similarities between the prayer of Mary and the prayer of Samuel's mother Hannah (**1 Samuel 2:1–10; Luke 1:46–55**). There is also a parallel between Samuel and Jesus (**1 Samuel 2:26; Luke 2:52**). Although it is never indicated that Jesus ever took the "Nazarite vow," He was *holy* and *separated* unto the Father in the deepest sense of the word. He was certainly not an ascetic in His lifestyle **(Matthew 9:11; Luke 15:1–2).**

3) The title *Branch*, or *netzer*, is given by the prophets like **Jeremiah 23:5, 33:15, and Zechariah 3:8, 6:12.** *"Then a 'shoot' will spring from the stem of Jesse, and a branch from his roots will bear fruit"* (**Isaiah 11:1–2; Revelation 22:16**).

Words with a similar sound have an overarching idea when we say words like *Nazareth, Nazarite,* or *Nazarene*. Yeshua was the *nezter,* (Branch) living in *notzri,* (Nazareth). The modern-day Hebrew word for "Christian" is *noztri*, because the first followers of Christ were called people of "the Way," or the way of the Nazarene (**Acts 9:2; John 14:6**).[4]

---

[4] This all may sound confusing and problematic but this is another proof that Matthew's gospel had to be originally written in the Hebrew tongue.

MATTHEW, THE HEBREW GOSPEL

Chapter Three

Matthew 3:1–3—*"In those days came John the Baptist, preaching in the wilderness of Judaea, And saying, Repent ye: for the kingdom of heaven is at hand. For this is he that was spoken of by the prophet Esaias, saying, The voice of one crying in the wilderness, Prepare ye the way of the Lord, make his paths straight."*

The silent years in Nazareth have sent many saints into ecstasy trying to understand why the Bible does not give us more about those childhood years of Jesus. All we have recorded is that *"the child grew, and waxed strong in spirit, filled with wisdom: and the grace of God was upon him"* (**Luke 2:40**). Then Luke also records the account where Jesus was twelve years old, when he was debating with the religious leaders in Jerusalem (**Luke 2:41–52**). We know that Jesus was raised in a Jewish family, and would have been taught the scriptures as a boy. It was documented by the Greek philosopher, Epictetus, (55–135 AD), that Jesus made *"plows and yokes,"* working with his father in the carpenter's shop. In the Hebrew, He was a *charash*, a craftsman of wood and stone. All of the houses in Jesus' day were made out of local stones, and the doors, plows, and many farming yokes were made out of the local wood.

But for the most part, the Holy Spirit did not choose to fill up the sacred text with the childhood days of our Lord. I think it was to keep the focus on His mission and why He really came into this world. If the Bible had a lot of the mundane things of Jesus' early years, we would have the tendency to be sentimental and lose our concentration on Who He really was. So now Matthew's gospel skips ahead to the time of the beginning of Jesus' earthly ministry and the one who was to prepare His entrance.

"In those days" is used often by the prophets of old to designate the Messianic Era and the time of Israel's restoration **(Isaiah 38:1; Jeremiah 3:16; Joel 2:29; Zechariah 8:6)**. Matthew may have been using this phrase to signal that the Messianic day had dawned, and that Israel's salvation was at hand.

"Came John the Baptist" or "Yochanan the Immerser." *Yochanan* means "Yahweh is gracious," and *Immerser* means the "Baptizer." We know from other accounts like **John 1:6**, that John was a man *"sent from God."* All we know about John is that he was *"the greatest man born of woman"* (**Matthew 11:11**). It's hard to fathom that John the Baptist was greater than Noah, or Abraham, or Moses, or Elijah, but he was the forerunner of Israel's Messiah. He was blessed to not only see Christ, but to prepare His way, and to baptize Christ as well. When the world looks at greatness, they see someone with great talent, or a sports figure, or a millionaire, or someone who has succeeded in business, but God sees greatness totally different than the world.

"Preaching in the wilderness of Judaea" In the deserts of Judaea is where many prophets were made, where godly men were sifted of all of their pride and vanity. About seventeen or eighteen miles east of Jerusalem north of the Dead Sea is a place of desolation—the lower Jordan Valley called "the wilderness of Judaea." Part of the territory is now present-day Jordan; in the gospel accounts it is called, "land beyond Jordan" and is also called the territory of Perea, governed by the tetrarch Herod Antipas. It may well be that the dwelling place of John in the desert, down at the Jordan River, was to emphasize a *re-entry* into the land as a *re-enactment* of Israel's original conquest of the land from the book of Joshua. The appearance of the kingdom of heaven would not be one of joy and comfort, like most of Israel expected, but by repentance. For four hundred long years, no prophet had thundered in Israel. Israel was expecting the Messiah to come with applause and to establish His kingdom on the earth. Most of the Gentiles would be excluded, they thought, but when John came the message was convicting and disturbing.

"Repent ye: for the kingdom of heaven is at hand." It was never said that John "preached the gospel" because he was never allowed to see the death, burial, and resurrection of the Messiah, but he preached repentance, or *teshuvah*, meaning, "to turn from one's sins and return to God." The Greek word for repentance only means "to change one's mind or thinking." This was commonly taught in the Old Testament, and can be seen in the life of wicked men like Manasseh, who turned to God while in his afflictions (**2 Chronicles 33:13**). Repentance is also a center element in the message of the Messiah when He begins His ministry in Galilee (**Matthew 1:17**). The kingdom of heaven was at hand and John's message was energized by the dawning of the age of the Messiah. The people's lives must change!

The term, "kingdom of heaven" or *malchut shamayim,* is synonymous with the term, "kingdom of God"; they are one and the same. The religious Jews would not speak God's name, so they used substitute names like "Heaven." The kingdom of heaven has an outer dimension as well as an inner dimension. The kingdom of heaven would have come physically in John's day if Israel had repented and accepted Yeshua as their Messiah, but that day was postponed until after the Church Age. So the kingdom of heaven came in a spiritual sense to all of those who did accept Yeshua, and who asked Him to rule in their hearts. This is still going on today; when a person turns from their sins and turns to Christ to rule their life, then the kingdom has come to them spiritually. We all pray and yearn with Israel, for that kingdom to come on the earth like the prophets and Jesus foretold (**Examples: Isaiah 11, 35, 43; Amos 9; Zechariah 14; Matthew 19:28; Romans 11:25–26; Revelation 20:6**). So the kingdom of heaven is a current reality as well as something that is yet coming in the future. The kingdom of heaven is a reoccurring term in Matthew's gospel as we will visit this beautiful thought many times throughout the book. *Are you in the kingdom, dear reader? Are you looking for the kingdom to come?*

"For this is he that was spoken of by the prophet Esaias." The prophet Isaiah even wrote about the forerunner of the Messiah in **Isaiah 40:3**. In the proper context, Isaiah is writing to give comfort to the Babylonian exiles, that God has not abandoned His people. The Lord is going to make a way for them to return to their land. The obstacles that stand in their way are going to be removed and the road home is being prepared. But the overarching picture is the comfort that the Messiah is going to bring to His people and the "voice" that will announce His coming. The true King is coming, **"make his paths straight."** In ancient times, when a king was coming through a country, the routes were cleared of anything that would hinder his travels. John the Baptist was not going to clear the natural obstacles out of the way but the spiritual obstacles inside the hearts of the people.

The prophets were inspired to write about the first and second comings of the Messiah, but they were not chosen to know the time He was to come (**1 Peter 1:10–11**). Daniel was an exception (**Daniel 9:25–26**). Other passages that referred to the messenger, or John the Baptist were: **Exodus 23:30 and Malachi 3:1.**

Matthew 3:4—*"And the same John had his raiment of camel's hair, and a leathern girdle about his loins; and his meat was locusts and wild honey."*

John's dress and diet were in direct opposition to the religious establishment of his day. This also connects him with the spirit of Elijah. Notice the comparison in their attire in **2 Kings 1:8**. Matthew is comparing the days of John the Baptist with the final arrival of the Messiah, when Elijah will come (**Malachi 4:5**). Many scholars have thought that the "locusts" were fruit from the carob tree. But after further review, there was a certain type of locust that was kosher for Jews to eat (**Leviticus 11:21–22**). The large grasshopper is still eaten by the Bedouins even today. "Wild honey" was not honey from bee hives, but the honey that came out of dates. The Judaean desert was filled with date trees. The point that Matthew is making is that John lived a simple life, and was not out to get money from the people like many false prophets did then and are still doing today.

Matthew 3:5–6—*"Then went out to him Jerusalem, and all Judaea, and all the region round about Jordan, And were baptized of him in Jordan, confessing their sins."*

What a phenomenon John was! There were no modern ways of communication such as television, radio, microphones, not even printing presses or newspapers to advertise, and yet people were coming from everywhere to hear John. Why is this? Because John had the power of God on his life, and they knew his message was true. There is no way that we can understand how powerful John's ministry was, being removed so far from the culture of his day.[5] Again, he was preparing the way for the coming Messiah, and many of these people that were attracted to John would later start following Jesus, and that was the intent.

---

[5] Every year when I travel to Israel, it never ceases to amaze me how dry and desolate southern Israel is compared to the beautiful Galilee in the north. As one travels from Jerusalem, at 2500 feet above sea level, he goes down, down, down, approximately twenty miles, to the lowest point on planet Earth, to the region of the Dead Sea, at 1300 feet below sea level. This geographical mystery was designed by the Creator to be the place where our Savior would show forth His humility. The lowest point on earth would be where Christ would identify Himself with sinful man. So we should not be surprised that the Messiah's forerunner would also have his ministry in the desert of Judaea.

"And were baptized of him in Jordan" Washing of the body was used in Jewish rituals as far back as **Genesis 35:2**: *"Then Jacob said unto his household, and to all that were with him, Put away the strange gods that are among you, and be clean, and change your garments."* Bathing in water was used to return a person to a state of ritual purity. Read **Leviticus 14, 15, 16; Numbers 19:11, 31:22–23.** The word *mikveh* is used in **Genesis 1:10** to describe a *"gathering of waters."* In **Exodus 7:19** and **Isaiah 22:11**, it means a *"reservoir of water."* In **Leviticus 11:36**, it denotes a *"gathering of water"* in a cistern. Even though it was never used to describe a place of ritual bathing, this is where the rabbis adopted the term. People living in Bible times may have used the word *mikveh* for "hope," as this is the word used in **Jeremiah 14:8** and **Jeremiah 17:13**. Living in the dry regions of the desert they considered the places of water a resting place along their journey.

Water immersion was also used in proselyte conversions. If a Gentile wanted to be converted to the God of Israel, a male would be circumcised and immersed in water to be identified with the God of Israel. A Gentile woman would only be immersed. But this became a major part of temple and synagogue worship in Bible times. The people would self-immerse themselves before entering into a place of worship. Archaeologists have uncovered many ritual baths at the southern steps of the temple in Jerusalem, and also at many of the synagogue ruins in Israel.

So John did not invent this idea of "baptism"; it had been used for centuries as a sign for ritual purity. John the Baptist was called by God to use water baptism as a means of identifying one's self with repentance. There was a Messianic fever in the air, the time had arrived, and John was the man that God raised up to call Israel back to God. Water baptism was <u>never</u> a means of salvation, like many churches have taught over the years; it was a means of "identification."

"Confessing their sins" This was commanded in places like **Leviticus 5:5** and **Numbers 5:6–7.** This word, "confess" or *yadah*, would have been used by our Lord in **Matthew 10:32**. The apostle Paul would later use the Greek word for confess, *homologeo*, in **Romans 10:9–10**. God gave us our mouths so we could feed our physical bodies and so that we could feed our spiritual bodies by confessing our sins, and acknowledging Jesus as Lord of our lives.

Matthew 3:7—*"But when he saw many of the Pharisees and Sadducees come to his baptism, he said unto them, O generation of vipers, who hath warned you to flee from the wrath to come?"*

It was a long, hard journey from the mountains of Jerusalem of over 2500 feet above sea level, through the ravines and gorges down to approximately 1300 feet below sea level, to the Jordan River, north of the Dead Sea. John's ministry was so powerful that he was attracting the religious leaders of his day. The Pharisees and Sadducees were not coming to repent of their sins, but to attack John. Religious imposters had no place in God's kingdom.

"O generation of vipers, who hath warned you to flee from the wrath to come?" Vipers are noted for the subtle approach, just like the serpent in **Genesis 3**. John knew that the authorities had not supported his message before so he said, *". . . <u>who</u> hath warned you to flee from the wrath to come?"* Hypocrisy is the worst kind of sin in the scriptures, especially when people are in a position to lead many others astray.

Matthew 3:8–9—*"Bring forth therefore fruits meet for repentance: And think not to say within yourselves, We have Abraham to our father: for I say unto you, that God is able of these stones to raise up children unto Abraham."*

John uses the metaphor of *fruit*, that is used many times in the Old Testament and Jesus used it as well (**Psalm 1; John 15**). The theology of the Pharisees and Sadducees was that because they came from the lineage of

Abraham, they would be granted blessing and protection in this world and the world to come. This blessing of Abraham was so strong that it was even carried over in Paul's writings to the Gentile believers **(Romans 4; Galatians 3)**. But the problem was, these Pharisees and Sadducees were not living the lives that matched their pedigree. Water baptism without true repentance is only an outward ritual.

"God is able of these stones to raise up children unto Abraham." God raised up the children of Israel by the miraculous birth of Isaac when Sarah was in her old age. The same metaphor of being raised up from rocks is used in **Isaiah 51:1–2:**

"Hearken unto me, ye that follow after righteousness, ye that seek the Lord: <u>look unto the rock whence ye are hewn,</u> and to the hole of the pit whence are digged. Look unto Abraham your father, and unto Sarah that bare you: for I called him alone, and blessed him, and increased him."

John the Baptist is cutting the ground out from under the religious authorities who claimed to stand in their own righteousness, rather than the righteousness that only the Messiah could give. God is calling the rulers of Israel to repentance in the same region where their forefathers had crossed over into the Promised Land. They would reject John's preaching, and would also reject Jesus as their Messiah, clinging also to the fact that they were descendants from Abraham **(John 8:33–40)**. None are so blind as the religious, who can play the part and hear the message and still not see their need for Christ!

Matthew 3:10—*"And now also the axe is laid unto the root of the trees: therefore every tree which bringeth not forth fruit is hewn down, and cast into the fire."*

One reason the fruit tree is used so much when God speaks of judgment is because fruit trees were vital to everyday life in Bible times. When Israel was attacking their enemies, they were told not to cut down the fruit trees, because they could eat of them (**Deuteronomy 20:19**). One of the most beautiful and mysterious wonders of God's creation is a fruit tree. God designed the fruit to have the seed in itself, which would grow another tree (**Genesis 1:11–12**). So here we have the forerunner of the Messiah, John the Baptist, using this metaphor of a fruit tree to describe judgment on those who are not bearing fruit. God is giving Israel a chance by calling them to repentance. A person who has true, biblical faith in Christ will produce a life of good works (**James 2**). If the works are not evident in their life, they were probably never saved in the first place.

The metaphor of the final judgment as a consuming fire was used by the prophets (**Isaiah 66:24; Joel 2:30; Malachi 4:1**). In the coming of the Messiah of Israel, the very Son of God, judgment had already begun.

Matthew 3:11—*"I indeed baptize you with water unto repentance: but he that cometh after me is mightier than I, whose shoes I am not worthy to bear: he shall baptize you with the Holy Ghost, and with fire."*

John's water baptism in the Jordan River was a symbol of repentance. But John puts himself in the lowest status of a slave when compared to the coming Messiah. ***"But he that cometh after me"*** is similar to the language we find in **Psalm 118:26, Genesis 49:10,** and **Song of Solomon 2:8**. The real baptism is going to be done by the Messiah: ***"he shall baptize you with the Holy Ghost, <u>and with fire</u>."*** It will be a *two-fold* baptism. For those who repent and follow the Messiah, they will be filled with the *Ruach Ha Qodesh*, or Holy Spirit, and the Spirit will purify them to be citizens of the kingdom of God. But those who refuse the Messiah, the baptism of fire will be one of judgment and condemnation.

Matthew, writing around **35–40 AD,** and after the day of Pentecost, which occurred around **32–33 AD,** knew that the Holy Spirit baptism was bestowed on His people later than the time of Jesus' death and resurrection.

Matthew 3:12—*"Whose fan is in his hand, and he will thoroughly purge his floor, and gather his wheat into the garner, but he will burn up the chaff with unquenchable fire."*

At the end of the harvest season, a farmer will bring the wheat into a threshing floor, which was a rock or hard-packed dirt surface, sometimes with a short wall around the perimeter. The farmer would then take a wooden pitchfork and toss the wheat up in the air, where the wind would blow the chaff away and leave only the wheat heads in the threshing floor. The wheat would be stored in the granary to be later used in making bread. The chaff would then be raked into piles and burned. This was a very common scene in Israel during the harvest season.

This metaphor of winnowing was also used by the prophets (**Isaiah 33:11; Psalm 1:4; Malachi 4:1**). John is saying that the Messiah owns the threshing floor, and the winnowing fork is in His hand. What a contrast! The *wheat* (believers) are gathered into the safe keeping of the Messiah, while the *chaff* (unbelievers) is burned up. Just try to imagine the power behind John's words that day on the bank of the Jordan River. I would have liked to have seen the faces of those Pharisees and Sadducees.

Matthew 3:13—*"Then cometh Jesus from Galilee to Jordan unto John, to be baptized of him."*

From Nazareth down to the region north of the Dead Sea is about seventy-five or eighty miles. It is believed that John never knew Jesus until this day, even though they were cousins (**John 1:31**). John may have known *about* Jesus, but it was not revealed to John that Jesus was the Messiah until now.

We know that Jesus was about thirty years old when He came to John to be baptized (**Luke 3:23; Numbers 4:3**). The priests in the Old Testament had to be thirty years old and Jesus the Messiah would be our Great High Priest, who would offer up Himself as a perfect sacrifice for the sins of His people (**Hebrews 5**).

Matthew 3:14–15— *"But John forbad him, saying, I have need to be baptized of thee, and comest thou to me? And Jesus answering said unto him, suffer it to be so now: for thus it becometh us to fulfill all righteousness. Then he suffered him."*

Once again, we see the humility of John the Baptist. When compared to the Son of God, John is a mere slave, and feels his unworthiness to water baptize the Messiah. Wow! Have you ever wondered how we will feel when we stand before the glorious Savior the very first time?

"Suffer it to be so now: for thus it becometh us to fulfill all righteousness." Here we have the very first words of Jesus recorded by Matthew, and they contain two important words, *"fulfill"* and *"righteousness."* The appearance of Israel's Messiah would fulfill what the prophets had written, and would give righteousness to sinful humanity. This is such a dramatic beginning to the earthly ministry of Christ that I feel a need to mention several suggestions:

1) The washing of the priests in the Old Testament served as a background to the baptism and consecration of the Messiah (Exodus 29:4).

2) Jesus was placing His stamp of approval on John's ministry.

3) Jesus was anticipating His own "baptism of death" (Luke 12:50), by which he would secure righteousness for His people.

4) The righteousness that John was preaching to the people about would be fulfilled by the Messiah.

5) Jesus was identifying Himself with sinful humanity, for the perfect Lamb of God had no sin (2 Corinthians 5:21).

6) Jesus was also setting an example for everyone who would follow Him to be baptized as a symbol of His death, burial, and resurrection.

Matthew 3:16–17— *"And Jesus, when he was baptized, went up straightway out of the water: and, lo, the heavens were opened unto* *him, and he saw the Spirit of God descending like a dove, and lighting upon him: And lo a voice from heaven, saying, This is my beloved Son, in whom I am well pleased."*

"Went up straightway out of the water" It seems to be clear that the word *baptize* means "to immerse." And even though water baptism was never intended to be a means of salvation, the biblical mode was by immersion. The other modes of baptism, and the doctrines of baptism regeneration, came along during the second and third centuries.

"The heavens were opened" This idea of the heavens opening as though the curtains of the divine dwelling were pulled aside, is used in **Psalm 104:2, Isaiah 40:22, Ezekiel 1:1, Acts 7:56, 10:11, and Revelation 11:19, 19:11.**

"He saw" John saw the Spirit of God not only descend on the Messiah, but the Spirit of God *"remained"* on Him (**John 1:33**). In the Old Testament, the Spirit of God would come upon the prophets but then He would leave. The sign to John that this truly was the long-awaited Messiah would be that the Spirit of God would *remain* on Him. The Spirit of God is given to all of God's children *by measure*, but it is said of Christ that **"God giveth not the Spirit by measure unto him"** (John 3:34).

"The Spirit of God descending like a dove, and lighting upon him." It's very interesting to me that in **Genesis 1:2**, we read, **"the Spirit of God moved, rachaph, on the waters."** The word *rachaph* is only used again in **Deuteronomy 32:11**, where the **"eagle fluttereth,** or *rachaph* **over her young."** The very same idea is given here when the Spirit of God hovered over the Messiah. In the beginning, the Spirit of God was bringing about a new creation, and at the baptism of the Messiah, the Spirit of God was once again bringing about a new creation. All who placed their sincere trust in Him would be made new creatures (**2 Corinthians 5:17**).

The verbiage of the *Spirit of God* anointing the Messiah is mentioned in places like **Isaiah 42:1** and **Isaiah 11:2**. Jesus said in the synagogue in Nazareth that *"the Spirit of God is upon me"* in **Luke 4:18.**

The *dove* was a symbol of sacrifice. As we can see when the Savior came into the world, his earthly parents offered turtle doves for a sacrifice in the temple (**Leviticus 12:8; Luke 2:24**). The Messiah would be the supreme sacrifice!

When Jesus was anointed with the Holy Spirit, this was the fulfillment of anointing the Old Testament priests with oil in **Exodus 29:7**.

"This is my beloved Son" Referring to **Psalm 2:7**. Two attestations that Yeshua was the Messiah, 1) the *Spirit*, 2) the *Father*. What a beautiful picture we have here of the triune Godhead. **God the Father** speaking from heaven, the **Son of God** in the river of Jordan, and the **Holy Spirit** descending upon Him.

"In whom I am well pleased." Referring to **Isaiah 42:1**. Pulling passages from two different verses was called, *"a string of pearls."* Jesus also used this method (**Matthew 22:37–39**).

This showed that the Father would accept the work of His Son on earth. The Son had come to do the Father's will, and the Spirit of God would help Him finish the mission. So we have the visible presence of the Holy Spirit and the audible voice of God Almighty at the baptism of the Messiah. This audible voice of the Father would be heard again at the Mount of Transfiguration in **Matthew 17:5**. Two of the most underrated moments in the life of the Messiah are His baptism and His transfiguration.

Jesus the Christ is the only way to the Father (**John 14:6**).

We are confronted today with the words of Matthew, for we too must decide for ourselves. Is He truly the Messiah?

Chapter Four

The Temptation of the Messiah

Before the Messiah could start His public ministry, He had to overcome Satan, or the "tempter," in the flesh. The fact that Jesus quotes scriptures three times from the book of Deuteronomy, places the entire setting in contrast to the wanderings of Israel in the desert for forty years.

Deuteronomy 8:2–3—*"And thou shalt remember all the way which the Lord thy God led thee these forty years in the wilderness, to humble thee, and to prove thee, to know what was in thine heart, whether thou wouldest keep his commandments, or no. And he humbled thee, and suffered thee to hunger, and fed thee with manna, which thou knewest not, neither did thy fathers know; that he might make thee know that man doth not live by bread only, but by every word that proceedeth out of the mouth of the Lord doth man live."*

Israel grumbled over the lack of food and gave into idolatry when they were tempted. But Yeshua the Messiah was victorious. The question has been asked, "Could the Messiah have sinned?" Once, a contractor and his crew built a huge concrete bridge over a river. After years of hard work and planning, the bridge was completed. They asked a heavy transport truck to cross the bridge first. When the truck passed to the other side, the contractor said, "We wanted the truck driver to drive his truck over the bridge to prove to everybody that the bridge <u>could not</u> fall." Jesus the Christ was tempted, not to show that He could sin, but to prove that He was above sin. But Satan still hurled his weapons on the Messiah throughout His ministry and even while He was on the cross.

Just as Israel was tempted after they came through the waters of the Red Sea, the Messiah was tempted after His baptism in the Jordan River. His forty days of fasting parallels Israel's forty years of wandering. Jesus is our model and our example, and because He won the victory we can live a life of victory over Satan. ***"The Lord trieth the righteous"*** (**Psalm 11:5a**). The Lord allows temptation to come into our lives to make us strong and valuable in His kingdom. A person who has lived a sheltered life, free from trouble, free from temptation, most of the time does not make a strong soldier. But the Christian who has been tried and tested may turn out to be the best worker in the kingdom.[6]

---

[6] I recall a pastor who told about a self-righteous woman in his church who was always criticizing the pretty young ladies in the church for their flirtatious ways. The older woman had never been married and she had not been blessed with the beauty of some of the younger girls. Her jealousy was causing her to always gossip about others when she had never been placed in the same situation. It's easy for us to condemn others when we have not walked in their shoes.

But Jesus was a perfect target for the devil because Satan knew that the world's salvation was in the balance, and that the Messiah was the only One who could provide eternal life. The devil's attack was on the *Man* Jesus, and he thought he could divert His attention away from the Father mission.

Matthew 4:1—*"Then was Jesus led up of the Spirit into the wilderness to be tempted of the devil."*

"Then Jesus was led up" The Jordan River empties into the north part of the Dead Sea, and that is believed to be the region where John baptized Jesus, the lowest point on planet Earth. Then Jesus was led *up* from that place, going back east, to a higher elevation.

"...led up of the spirit" The Holy Spirit led the Messiah into being tempted by the devil. Some people think that the Spirit only leads into a place of comfort and safety. But many times God's presence takes us into a place of limited testing, a place where our character and faith can be proven. God never leads us where He will not help us through the trial. I love the passage in the life of Moses, when God was leading the children of Israel and calling Moses to be the leader. Moses told the Lord:

"If thy presence go not with me, carry us not up hence" (Exodus 33:15).

I had rather be in a temptation *with* God's presence than to be living comfort and ease *without* God's presence. Because where God leads, He will make a way to endure (**1 Corinthians 10:13**).

"...into the wilderness" Speaking of the Judaean desert in southern Israel. The desert is where God molded men like Abraham, Moses, Elijah, and John the Baptist. The Messiah would be the Prophet, like unto Moses (**Deuteronomy 18:15**). Above Jericho today, there is a mountain called the Mount of Temptation, where tradition says that Jesus was taken by the devil. This is probably not the exact spot, but it is a place to reflect on the Messiah's temptation, and can be seen for miles as you travel through the Jordan Valley.

"...to be tempted of the devil" In **Genesis 3:15**, we read: ***"and I will put enmity between thee and woman, and between thy seed and her seed."*** The "seed of the woman" (Jesus) would defeat the "seed of the serpent" (devil). All through the history of Israel, Satan tried to kill the seed of the woman. The devil could not prevent the Redeemer from coming into the world, but that did not stop the devil from trying to thwart the Messiah's mission after He was born into the world.

The devil is not some evil force in the air; he is a real, spiritual being that is the archenemy of God and His people. He has a well-organized army of evil beings who are in control of this present world system. The devil is also a religious being, and his number one weapon of warfare is religion. Why would he come against the very Son of God if he was not concerned about God's kingdom? The devil's workshop is filled with religious tools. What a thought—*The Messiah* was tempted of the *devil!*

Matthew 4:2—*"And when he had fasted forty days and forty nights, he was afterward an hungered."*

Moses fasted for forty days and forty nights in **Exodus 34:28.** The point is, that Jesus was left without physical strength, and He had to rely totally on the Spirit for help. Again, Jesus did not face the devil as a divine superhuman, but as a Man who relied on the Holy Spirit to fight the battle. What an example for us to follow.[7]

---

[7] If I may give another example: Suppose a train was coming at top speed down the railroad tracks, and someone was standing on the tracks with outstretched arms. The train would not even register the impact, and the man would be knocked off in a split second. But if the man was able to stop the train, not only would the train be stopped, but the man would feel the full force of the oncoming train. Jesus knew the full force of temptation. He has felt everything that you and I feel in this life, but He stopped the train, Hallelujah!

Three categories of temptation:
1) Lust of the Flesh
2) Lust of the Eyes
3) The Pride of Life (**Genesis 3; 1 John 2:16**).

Lust of the Flesh and Lust of the Eyes

Matthew 4:3—*"And when the tempter came to him, he said, If thou be the Son of God, command that these stones be made bread."*

Because Jesus was so weak physically, after the long fast, the devil's offer was to fulfill His physical needs by divine power. One may ask, "How could that be wrong?" Satan was trying to get Jesus to use His divine power in a way that was not consistent with God the Father's reason for sending Him into the world. It was part of the humility of the Messiah, not abusing His divine power. *The devil tempted Jesus the same way he tempts us—satisfy the flesh first.*

"If thou be the Son of God" Notice the devil was attacking the deity of the Messiah. The number one reason we have the gospel accounts is so that we might believe that Jesus is the Christ, the Son of God (**John 20:31; 1 John 5:5, 5:10–13**).

Always be watchful. Satan will always try to undermine the deity of Christ. Was Jesus just a prophet? Was Jesus just a miracle worker? Was Jesus just an historical figure? Did Jesus just start a new religious movement? This is the point that Matthew is driving home to his readers; Jesus was the Messiah of Israel, the Son of the living God!

"…command that these stones be made bread" Israel demanded bread in the wilderness and died. Yeshua denied Himself physical bread, and yet He is the Bread of life (**John 6:35**). Jesus said, *"I have meat to eat that ye know not of"* (**John 4:32**)*.* Try to imagine doing without bread for forty days, and having the power to turn stones into bread. *The devil tempted Jesus the same way he tempts us—have what your eyes can see.*

Matthew 4:4— *"But he answered and said, It is written, Man shall not live by bread alone, but by every word that proceedeth out of the mouth of God."*

"It is written" Written where? Jesus is quoting from **Deuteronomy 8:3** from the *TNKH,* which is an acronym for the first letters of the three parts of the Hebrew scriptures:

1) ***TORAH,*** (First five book of Moses—Genesis, Exodus, Leviticus, Numbers, and Deuteronomy)

2) ***N'VI'IM,*** (Prophets—Joshua, Judges, Samuel, Kings, Isaiah, Jeremiah, Ezekiel, and the twelve minor prophets)

3) ***K'TUVIM,*** (Historical writings—Psalms, Proverbs, Job, Song of Songs, Ruth, Lamentations, Ecclesiastes, Esther, Daniel, Ezra, Nehemiah, and Chronicles)

In what we call the Old Testament, the word will be *cepher* or "book or scroll." In the gospel accounts it is rendered, *"scriptures"* like in **Matthew 21:42**, or *"book"* like in **Luke 4:17, 20**.

Notice the words *"mouth of God."* We survive physically by eating bread with our mouths, but the way Jesus defeated the devil was by the words that proceeded out of the *mouth of God*. We fail to realize the supernatural power that is in God's word. If we would only digest His word into our lives, like God told Ezekiel to do in **Ezekiel 3:1**, then we could defeat Satan. We need to be people of the scriptures!

Pride of Life

Matthew 4:5–7—*"Then the devil taketh him up into the holy city, and setteth him on a pinnacle of the temple, And saith unto him, If thou be the Son of God, cast thyself down: for it is written, he shall give his angels charge concerning thee: and in their hands they shall bear thee up, lest at any time thou dash thy foot against a stone. Jesus said unto him, It is written, Thou shalt not tempt the Lord thy God."*

"…holy city" Jerusalem (**Nehemiah 11:1; Isaiah 48:2; Daniel 9:24**); *"…pinnacle of the temple"* Believed to be the southwest corner of the temple compound. Archaeologists have found a stone, fallen from the top of the southwest corner wall with the engraving of where the shofar was blown to announce the Jewish feasts and Sabbath days. This would have been the highest point.

"If thou be the Son of God, cast thyself down" Again, Satan is trying to make fun of the deity of the Messiah with the word *"if."* The devil was simply tempting Jesus to draw attention to Himself by falling headlong off of the pinnacle of the temple, and then calling for the angels to catch Him before he hit the ground below. Satan takes the real meaning of **Psalm 91:11–12,** out of context. The true context of **Psalm 91**, is that of those who live their lives in faithful obedience to the Heavenly Father, they will be blessed and protected. But the devil is trying to turn that which was righteous into sin. *The devil tempted Jesus the same way he will tempt us—draw attention to yourself.*

Satan has been using false prophets for centuries to misplace the scriptures. When you hear someone preach the Bible, make sure they do not take the scriptures out of context and make them say something different than what God intended for them to say. Denominational teachings are notorious for misplacing scripture. This is one of the main reasons why most churches are in spiritual confusion today.

"It is written again, Thou shalt not tempt the Lord thy God." Jesus is quoting from **Deuteronomy 6:16**. God protects His children, but we are not to test the Lord by trying to make Him do anything. Preserving one's life is part of the commandments of God. There are natural laws that God has placed in the universe and we are tempting God when we presume that God will perform a miracle on our behalf. In many cases, the "signs and wonders" movement of today runs contrary to the command of scripture. This does not nullify the miraculous power of God in our lives.

Matthew 4:8–10—*"Again, the devil taketh him up into an exceeding high mountain, and sheweth him all the kingdoms of the world, and the glory of them; And said unto him, all these things will I give thee, if thou wilt fall down and worship me. Then saith Jesus unto him, get thee hence Satan: for it is written, Thou shalt worship the Lord thy God, and him only shalt thou serve."*

"An exceeding high mountain" This may or may not be the high mountain east of Jericho called the Mount of Temptation. Matthew may be giving us a parallel to **Matthew 28:16–18**, where the risen Messiah took his disciples on a mountain in Galilee to tell them, *"All power is given unto me in heaven and earth."* Or Matthew might be reminding us of when God took Moses up on Mt. Pisgah, and showed him all the land of Israel (**Deuteronomy 34:1–4**).

Satan was tempting the Messiah to gain control of the entire world system, without going to the cross. The devil has the power to give us success in the world without serving the Lord. One of the big traps that people fall into is knowing that they can achieve worldliness and riches without knowing Christ. A person does not have to know Christ or serve Christ to have success in this world (**Psalm 73**). Satan is very subtle and cunning. He is in control of this present evil world (**1 John 5:19**).

But Jesus the Messiah saw the world in need of a Savior, and He came to seek and to save that which was lost, not to gain the world (**Matthew 8:20, 16:26; Luke 19:10**). He knew that one day He would establish the Davidic kingdom and then He would be the King over all the earth (**Zechariah 14:9**).

"If thou wilt fall down and worship me, . . . Get thee hence Satan: for it is written, Thou shalt worship the Lord thy God, and him only shalt thou serve." False worship was the downfall of Israel in the Old Testament. Jesus said of the religious leaders of His day, ***"Ye are of your father the devil"*** (**John 8:44a, 8:38**). If they had of been true worshipers of God, they would have known their Messiah.

The Messiah would not bow down to the devil. The *"god of this world"* (**2 Corinthians 4:4),** would be defeated by going to the cross. He came to do the Father's will. The demise of the devil would come through the uplifted Messiah on the tree in Jerusalem (**Matthew 16:23, 26:53–54; Colossians 2:14–15; Hebrews 2:14–15).**

Jesus is quoting from **Deuteronomy 6:13**, and Satan has no option but to yield to the power of the scriptures. Again, this is why we need to not only know the scriptures, but apply them to our everyday lives. Satan cannot stand against the truth of God's word. The word of God is our ultimate weapon (**Ephesians 6:17**).

Matthew 4:11—*"Then the devil leaveth him, and, behold, angels came and ministered unto him."*

"Then the devil leaveth him" The devil did not leave the Messiah alone, but he left *"for a time."*

"...behold, angels came" Matthew uses the word ***"behold,"*** signaling not only the end of the trial, but also the victory. And angels probably gave the Messiah food, like the angels fed Elijah in **1 Kings 19:5–8**.

If God provided manna in the wilderness for the children of Israel, how much more would He provide food for His Son in the wilderness?

Before we leave this crucial episode in the life of Christ, let's reflect on three important truths:

1) Satan's power is limited.

2) The scripture's power limits the devil.

3) The Spirit's power is unlimited.

Jesus the Messiah Begins His Galilean Ministry

Matthew 4:12—*"Now when Jesus had heard that John was cast into prison, he departed into Galilee."*

Matthew places the first part of the ministry of the Messiah in Galilee, while John's gospel gives the first part in the Messiah's ministry in Judaea. There is no contradiction; it's just that John was writing many years later to a different audience and it includes the time when Jesus and John's ministry overlapped.

The first-century historian, Flavius Josephus (37-100 AD), wrote about the ministry of John. He recorded that Herod Antipas put John in prison down at Machaerus, on the eastern side of the Dead Sea. Matthew does not give the reason John was cast into prison until **Matthew 14.**

The crowds that had been following John would now follow Jesus, and that was the intent all along, as John says in **John 3:30.** We will learn more about John and his ministry when we get to **Matthew 11.**

"He departed into Galilee." Herod Antipas was the tetrarch of Galilee and Perea, on the east side of the Jordan River. Jesus also knew that He only had a small window of time for His ministry. He would depart into different regions, knowing that danger was lurking. It helps us to be reminded that the constant danger from the time the Messiah was born, throughout His ministry, to His death in Jerusalem, was all in the divine hands of the Father, sending His Son into the world *"in the fulness of time"* **(Galatians 4:4)**. God was using the Herod Dynasty and Romans, and the corrupt Jewish establishment, and they didn't even know it.

Matthew 4:13–16[8]—*"And leaving Nazareth, he came and dwelt in Capernaum, which upon the sea coast, in the borders of Zabulon and Nephthalim: That it might be fulfilled which was spoken by Esaias the prophets, saying, The land of Zabulon, and the land of Nephthalim, by the way of the sea, beyond Jordan, Galilee of the Gentiles; The people which sat in darkness saw great light; and to them which sat in the region and shadow of death light is sprung up."*

"And leaving Nazareth, he came and dwelt in Capernaum" Nazareth is approximately seventeen to eighteen miles southwest of the Sea of Galilee. Even though Jesus grew up in Nazareth, His hometown for His ministry would be Capernaum. Capernaum, or *Kefar Nahum,* "village of consolation," was on the northern shore of the lake. It is believed to have had a population of around 1,000 to1,500 in the time of Jesus. They have discovered about a 2,500-foot promenade with several piers that extended out into the water from Capernaum in Jesus' time. This was used in the fishing business as well as a transportation center for crossing the sea.

---

[8] I have to say that we are entering into some of my favorite passages of scripture. Having traveled to Israel for many years, there is no place on Earth that touches my heart like Galilee. So for several chapters you may feel some of my personal feelings as we walk with our Lord along the hillsides of Galilee.

When you go there today, you will see the remains of a fourth-century synagogue that was built on top of the original foundation of the first-century synagogue from the time of Christ, built by the Roman centurion (**Luke 7:5**). Peter's house was discovered just a stone's throw away, and it is believed to have been the location of one of the first Messianic congregation in the first century. A Byzantine church was built over Peter's house in the fifth century, and today a Franciscan, Catholic Church stands above Peter's house. Capernaum is one of the most visited places you will go in Israel.[9] You can see the black, basalt ruins of first-century houses with archaeological findings from different periods of time, many from the time of Jesus. Among the numerous findings from the first century, you can see an original olive press with a millstone, which was used in the time of Jesus.

"That it might be fulfilled" Jesus left Nazareth and came down to Capernaum, so the scriptures of **Isaiah 9:1–2** might be fulfilled. **Isaiah 9:1–7** was definitely considered to be a Messianic passage. When Jesus passed through the Valley of the Doves, and saw the Arbel cliffs, no doubt He knew that He was fulfilling the prophecy that Isaiah wrote about concerning the place that He was to have His ministry.

"The land of Zabulon and the land of Nephthalim" Nazareth was in the region of *Zabulon* and Capernaum was in the region known as

---

[9] Several years ago, when tourism was low in Israel, we were filming a television special. With no tourists to be seen, I was privileged to spend several hours in Capernaum one day by myself. Even though we must be careful and not romanticize the place, it was a moment-of-a-lifetime experience just to be able to spend some quiet time where my Lord once lived. Normally, tour buses have to struggle to find a parking place.

Nephthalim. These were the two tribes of Israel that settled in the northernmost region near the Sea of Galilee. It is interesting that the very first tribes that were taken into exile were Zabulon and Naphtali. Galilee is even mentioned in **2 Kings 15:29**. This is probably the reason why Galilee was a place of bad reputation. The argument was recorded that no prophet could come out of Galilee (**John 1:46, 7:41–42, 7:52**). But the Light of the Messiah would first be seen in this region.

"By the way of the sea" There was an ancient trade route dating from the Bronze Age (around 3000 BC), *the Via Maris*, which is Latin for, "the way of the sea." This comes from the Latin Vulgate translation of the scriptures. In the time of Jesus, it may have been called, "the Way of the Philistines" because it ran up the Coastal Plain, formerly Philistine territory. It reached from Egypt to Mesopotamia, connecting the two important political and cultural centers of the eastern world. Israel was the geographical land bridge connecting Africa, Asia, and Europe. This *Via Maris* trade route ran along the northern shore of Galilee before turning and going northward up to Damascus. The other major trade route was the King's Highway (**Numbers 20:17**), which ran farther east. The ministry of the Messiah would be carried by word of mouth on these major trade routes, and the news of His miracles would spread into other nations in a very short time. Again, the time of His coming was precisely on schedule.

"Galilee of the Gentiles" Since the time of the Assyrian campaign in 732 BC, this region had long experienced forced population of Gentiles. The Jewish people of Galilee were surrounded by non-Jewish people. In the time of Jesus, Tiberias, the capital, was on the west side, and was the home of Herod Antipas. It was unlawful for a religious Jew to go to Tiberias because it was built over a Jewish cemetery. On the southeast side of the lake was the Decapolis(ten cities), on the northeast was the Golan Heights (Bethsaida was one of the cities), and in the far north was the region of Caesarea Philippi, ruled by Herod Philip. So when Jesus came to the northern shore of Galilee, to places like Capernaum, there was a group of Jewish peasants, fishermen, and farmers who were surrounded by paganism. This will help you to understand why it was called *"Galilee of the Gentiles."*

"The people which sat in darkness saw great light; and to them which sat in the region and shadow of death light is sprung up."

This is a continuation of the fulfillment of **Isaiah 9:1–2**. Why do the scriptures call Galilee *"the region and shadow of death"*?

Because the people were being oppressed politically by the Romans and religiously by the scribes and Pharisees. Extreme heavy taxation by the Romans made everyday life a struggle to survive. The synagogues were following the teachings of the rabbis more than they were following the true teachings of the scriptures. The common people had nowhere to turn. Strong demonic activity was in Galilee, crippled people were coming from all around seeking relief of physical pain in the many hot springs that were in the area.

But the good news is, *"the people which sat in darkness saw great light."* The Messiah of Israel, the Son of God, had come to them in human flesh. The *"Light of the world"* (**John 8:12**), would shine forth in their midst, with hope and compassion. Think of the facial expressions of sadness that were turned to joy when they saw the lovely Lord Jesus? Even though the religious establishment rejected Jesus as their Messiah, many of the common people knew Who He was, and they loved Him (**Mark 12:37**).[10]

---

[10] I would like to think that I would have followed Christ if I had of lived in Galilee long ago, but that is not an easy question to answer. I'm glad that I was born in a time and place where I had enough light given to me that I did surrender to Him!

Matthew 4:17—*"From that time Jesus began to preach, and to say, Repent: for the kingdom of heaven is at hand."*

"Preach, and to say" is a Hebrew Semitism; it is not describing two different functions. The message of the Messiah was the same as the message of John the forerunner: "Repent" or *teshuvah,* meaning turn from your sins and return to God. The modern-day gospel that is being preached is not one of repentance; it is *"another gospel"* (**Galatians 1:8–9**). Today is all about prosperity and fulfilling one's dreams, but a gospel without the message of repentance is not the true gospel of Christ.

The kingdom of heaven was not coming later; it was *"at hand."* One of the strange and mysterious truths of the ministry of the Messiah is that if Israel had accepted Jesus as their Messiah, the physical kingdom would have been set up then. So Jesus was offering them the physical kingdom. Because Israel rejected their Messiah, the kingdom of God would come into the hearts of His followers spiritually, and the physical kingdom would be postponed until a later time.

Matthew 4:18–22—*"And Jesus, walking by the sea of Galilee, saw two brethren, Simon called Peter, and Andrew his brother, casting a net into the sea: for they were fishers. And he saith unto them, Follow me, and I will make you fishers of men. And they straightway left their nets, and followed him. And going on from thence, he saw other two brethren, James the son of Zebedee, and John his brother, in a ship with Zebedee their father, mending their nets; and he called them. And they immediately left the ship and their father, and followed him.*

It will help us to understand the mindset of a religious Jewish mother in the first century before trying to explain the text. The desire of a Jewish mother would be that she would have a "male" child, because he might be the Messiah. If she had a male child and he was not the Messiah, then it would be the mother's desire and prayer that some great rabbi, like Shammai, or Hillel, or Gamaliel, would call her son to be his student, or *talmid*. Evidently, the rabbis did not see anything noteworthy about Peter and Andrew and Zebedee's children. Religion always looks "inside the box" but the place to look is "outside the box" for disciples of Jesus. Our Lord saw something in these men that He could use. Maybe they were not tainted with Judaism, like the traditional religious people of the day. Jesus knew they would fall and stumble in their faith, but He also knew that one day they would change the course of the world. Jesus knew all about these men before He called them.

"And Jesus, walking by the sea of Galilee" What a thought! The very Son of God walking by the Sea of Galilee, hearing the water slosh up on the rocks, feeling the wind blow in His face, surrounded by the beautiful mountains and hills that are on both sides of the sea, with the farmers working in the fields that cover the northern shore, and then seeing the fishermen at work. This was a day that these fishermen would never forget.

"Saw two brethren, Simon called Peter, and Andrew his brother, casting a net into the sea: for they were fishers. And he saith unto them, follow me, and I will make you fishers of men."

Andrew had been a disciple of John the Baptist, and then when he started following Jesus, he went and found his brother Peter (**John 1:40–41**). Peter and Andrew were casting a circular net into the water with small weights made out of stone attached to the edge of the net. There are two important truths here about the way Matthew describes their new life that Jesus was calling them into:

1) The metaphor *"fishers of men"* (not a well-used metaphor) was meant to say, instead of catching fish they would catch men.
2) This would be a breaking away from their everyday affairs.

When Jesus said *"follow me,"* this meant that He would be their provider, as they sat at His feet and listened to His teachings. They would follow Jesus along the dusty roads of Galilee, seeing the miracles and hearing those beautiful parables. I have thought many times what it must have been like to have been one of the close disciples of Jesus, and little did they know what monumental moments were coming in the months ahead. They would see the gospel demonstrated in the life of the Messiah.

"I will make you fishers of men" These disciples were trained to be fishermen, and it took a lot of knowledge of the sea and its surroundings in order to be a good fishermen. But to be a *"fisher of men"* was something that only Jesus could train them to be. One of the major problems that we have created in our religious culture is to think that a classroom education in some Bible college will equip someone to be a preacher of the gospel. Again, Jesus has to make us fishers of men. We have to have His calling, His power, and His Spirit, not our own abilities and talents.

"And they straightway left their nets, and followed him" The calling to be a disciple of Jesus was so strong that they left their jobs to follow the preacher from Nazareth. This denotes faith and obedience. They sacrificed their jobs to conform to the Master's way of life. This is a pattern that we all must follow if we are to be true disciples.

"James the son of Zebedee, and John his brother" James comes from the Hebrew word, *Yaacov,* and John comes from the word *Yochanan.* Zebedee, or *Zavdai,* must have had mixed feelings when Jesus called his sons to follow him. But I'm sure that later he was rejoicing. The name Zebedee was found written on a column from the fifth century in Capernaum. The historical truth of this important family name had been handed down for centuries following.

We should not leave out their mother, who is identified as *Salome* (**Mark 16:1**; **Matthew 20:20**), which comes from the Hebrew word *shalom,* or "peace." Peace must have filled her heart when the great rabbi called her two sons.

James was later killed by Herod Agrippa I, around 43 AD, recorded in **Acts 12:2**. John would be the only disciple that would live to be old and die of natural causes. He would be the one that would be given the book of the Revelation of Jesus Christ on the isle of Patmos, around 95 AD.

"And they immediately left the ship and their father, and followed him" Leaving both their family and their occupation re-emphasizes the urgency and the Spirit of God that was in the call to follow the Son of God. There was no apprehensiveness, no waiting until tomorrow; the divine call called for a direct response. I'm reminded of the verse in **Matthew 10:37a:** *"He that loveth father or mother more than me is not worthy of me."*

Have you, dear reader, ever felt the call of God on your life? I answered that call years ago, and I can honestly tell you that I could never be satisfied in this life without serving Christ. I feel unworthy, unqualified, and many times my efforts are very feeble, but just to be a small part of His great work is the highest honor that I could ever have in this life. So if you ever feel that call, I encourage you to surrender. I have never regretted it, and I know these disciples of Galilee never got over what seemed to be just another working day, when Jesus of Nazareth walked by the shore and chose them to be His disciples.

Matthew 4:23—*"And Jesus went about all Galilee, teaching in their synagogues, and preaching the gospel of the kingdom, and healing all manner of sickness and all manner of disease among the people."*

Yeshua, the Jewish Messiah, went into the religious Jewish places of worship throughout all Galilee. Jesus knew that the religious leaders were not following Him, but he tried to reform their synagogues. His mission was to the lost sheep of the house of Israel (**Matthew 10:6**). Jesus' ministry would contrast the ministry of John the Baptist. John would stay in the desert, while Jesus would go to the people. *"All Galilee"* tells us that the Messiah went to the synagogue at Gamala, Chorazin, Capernaum, Arbel, Nazareth, (**Luke 4:16**), Magdala, and many others. The oldest one ever found is in Gamala, just northeast of the Sea of Galilee.

"Teaching in their synagogues, and preaching the gospel of the kingdom" What Bible was Jesus the Messiah using in the synagogues? He was using the Hebrew Tanach, written on a scroll. As we have already mentioned, the Hebrew scriptures were divided into three sections: Torah (books of Moses), Ne'Viim (the prophets), and Ke'Tuvim (Psalms and historical writings like Ruth, Job, etc.). This is the way Jesus would have taught the scriptures, bringing out those Messianic passages that were talking about Himself. Jesus was preaching about the kingdom—that believing in Him as their Messiah was the entrance into God's kingdom—and teaching about the way a kingdom person was supposed to live. But it wasn't long before the religious establishment ran Jesus out of their synagogues, why? Because He exposed their hypocrisy. His synagogue would later become the open air, the hillsides of Galilee, and even a boat on several occasions.

"Healing all manner of sickness and all manner of disease among the people" We know that John the Baptist performed no miracles (**John 10:41**). But the Messiah's ministry would be accompanied by physical miracles. The scripture says, *"all manner of sickness, and all manner of disease."* Jesus did not screen the sick like modern-day faith healers; He healed whatever the sickness or disease was. Of all the woes and physical ailments that sin had brought into the world through Satan, the Promised Seed of the woman had come to show His power to reverse.

Matthew 4:24–25—*"And his fame went throughout all Syria: and they brought unto him all sick people that were taken with divers diseases and torments, and those which were possessed with devils, and those which were lunatick, and those that had the palsy; and he healed them. And there followed him great multitudes of people from Galilee, and from Decapolis, and from Jerusalem, and from Judaea, and from beyond Jordan."*

The four-hundred-year silence between the Old and New Testaments had been broken by John the Baptist thundering in the Judaean wilderness, and now the silence was really broken with the appearance of the long-awaited Messiah of Israel. Though Yeshua never left the land of Israel during His ministry, His influence quickly spread beyond Israel's borders, even north to Syria. What a sight that must have been! There were no modern ways of communication, and yet the people were coming from everywhere to hear and to see Jesus; how could this be? Because Jesus was truly the Son of God, and the Holy Spirit was drawing people. The word of His ministry spread like wild fire along the major caravan routes; the streets of the towns and villages were filled with peasants, farmers, and merchants talking about the preacher from Nazareth.

There are many verses in Isaiah that talk about physical healings, like **Isaiah 29:18, 35:5–6, and 42:18**. But it is difficult to find verses that talk about casting out demons. These miracles were "Messianic miracles," miracles that proved that Jesus was truly the Messiah. **"Lunatick"** comes from the Latin word, *luna* or "moon," and many thought that epilepsy was caused by the moon. There was a strong connection between epilepsy and demonic possession, and that is why Matthew mentions these together. The kingdom of God had come, and the kingdom of darkness could not prevail.

"Galilee . . . Decapolis . . . Jerusalem . . . Judaea . . . beyond Jordan" Keeping in mind the way that most people traveled in the first century was on foot makes this passage even more interesting. It's roughly eighty or ninety miles from southern Israel to the Galilee, or about a three-day's journey. One sweet Catholic lady told me one day that she walked from Nazareth to Jerusalem in three days. The region of **Galilee** covered all of the area south and north of the Sea of Galilee, and people were following Christ from all of the towns and villages. The ***Decapolis***, (ten cities) was on the eastern side of the lake; it was a pagan territory that was mostly comprised of a mixed population of Hellenized Jews and Gentiles. The capital of the Decapolis was Scythopolis. The scriptures tell us that many of the religious people came up from ***Jerusalem***, always trying to trap Jesus with their questions, but many common people made the long walk up to Galilee from the holy city of Jerusalem to see Jesus. ***Judaea*** is the entire region around Jerusalem, including the desert. ***Beyond Jordan,*** was the region east of the Jordan River, known as Perea, which was governed by Herod Antipas in those days. This geographical picture that Matthew is giving us is a sign that this Messiah would bless the nations, like God promised to Abraham. His ministry would begin in Israel, but would eventually touch the entire world. Wow!

Chapter Five

Introduction to the Sermon on the Mount

Because there has been so much misinterpretation about this passage of scripture, I feel the need to prepare the way somewhat before we dive into the text. Up until this point, the words of Jesus have been limited, and Matthew has been introducing the King Messiah as Jesus or Yeshua, and referring to the beginning of His ministry in Galilee. So now that the King has been introduced, Matthew gives us the message of the King, and the people who belong to His kingdom.

The Sermon on the Mount, as it has been called, *is not the gospel, and is not the plan of salvation for the ages.* The gospel is the death, burial, and resurrection of Christ. Matthew 5–7 lays down the characteristics of the people who are in the *malkut shamayim,* or the kingdom of heaven. What distinguishes a kingdom person from the rest of the world? This is a spiritual test to see if we are truly children of God.

The Sermon on the Mount is closely related to the Old Testament, but the message that the Messiah is bringing is radically different. The last message of the Old Testament ended with a warning of a curse (**Malachi 4:6**). The New Testament begins with a series of blessings. The Law of Moses reveals the need of sinful man to have a Savior, while the New Testament provides the Savior. These three chapters struck violently against the Jewish traditions of the day. A new day had dawned, a new revelation had come, the way a person would be blessed was not by self-effort, or self-righteousness, but through receiving God's Son and His righteousness.

Galilee was noted for stirring up revolts (**Acts 5:37**), and the Zealots hid out in the caves in the Arbel cliffs and in the steep mountains of Gamala, which means "camel back." They were expecting a Messiah to be a military and political leader to set them free from the yoke and bondage of Rome (**John 6:15, 18:36**). But when the Messiah gave this powerful sermon, it was not about social reform or politics; it was about the inner soul of man, not external religion, morality, or politics. Jesus' concern was, and still is, about who we are, because who we are determines what we do.

The Sermon on the Mount runs contrary to the modern world's way of thinking. The world focuses on success, money, power, being a sports hero, or being famous in Hollywood. But Jesus declared that John the Baptist was the greatest man born of women. He had no possessions, no home, lived in the desert, dressed in camel's hair, and ate wild locusts and honey. He was not a part of the religious system of the day. He was a misfit and a failure, and yet he received the Lord's highest praise. In God's kingdom, things are not the way they seem. The rich don't always win, the well known may not be big in God's eyes. The big preachers and big ministries may not even be of God; they may be false prophets in disguise. Man looks on the outward appearance, but God looks at the heart (**1 Samuel 16:7**).

Jesus the Messiah was not a member of either one of the religious groups of His day; He was a Man of the people, and He was the perfect example of His own teachings. He lived what He said, and through His power we can follow His example.

In God's kingdom, things are reverse; it is the humble, the meek, the merciful, the pure in heart, and the peacemakers who are great, not the proud. The *beatitude* means the "attitude" of kingdom people, the right attitude toward God and His people. There again, it's not a question of theology or philosophy; it's what on the inside of a person. **"For I say unto you, That except your righteousness shall exceed the righteousness of** *the scribes and Pharisees, ye shall in no case enter into the kingdom of heaven"* (Matthew 5:20).

When we read through this important passage of scripture, you may feel unworthy; you may feel like you have failed in God's plan. But that is part of the purpose of it. The Sermon on the Mount is law, but it is the law taken to a higher level. What motivates us to do what we do? What are we when no one is looking? What is the condition of our hearts toward God and His people? The standards are much too high, and this necessitates the born-again experience. This passage makes us run to Jesus for mercy. But if we run to Jesus, receive His forgiveness, and live a life being filled with His love, then we shall be blessed. And there is no greater witness than for a person to see Christ in us. We can attend church services all of our lives and never show others Jesus. What subjects do we talk about the most around others? What kind of language do we use? Are we a forgiving person or do we hold grudges against others? How do we feel about money? Are we stingy or are we generous? Do we pray in private, or do we always try to put on a spiritual show?

This Sermon on the Mount was probably the greatest sermon that Jesus ever gave on how to live. I pray that all of us will have *"ears to hear what thus saith the Lord"*!

Matthew 5:1–2—*"And seeing the multitudes, he went up into a mountain: and when he was set, his disciples came unto him: And he opened his mouth, and taught them, saying,"*

There is a mountain that lies just north of the Sea of Galilee, where tradition says is the place where Jesus delivered this sermon. It happens to be one of my personal favorite places to visit in the Holy Land. It is a place where you have a beautiful view of the sea with the mountains on the east and west. You can see many different types of fruit crops, such as bananas, oranges, and avocados that grow along the hillsides that slope down to the water. On top of the Mount of Beatitudes is a wonderful place to get in touch with nature, see the flowers, and hear the birds that Jesus used as metaphors in His teachings. It touches me deeply to think that our Lord used the open air for His cathedral. What blessings we mere worldlings miss by limiting God to a building.

Multitudes were now following the Messiah, and when He saw the crowds, He decided to go up on the mountain and sit down. This was the proper poster for a Jewish teacher in Bible times. There probably was a subgroup of "disciples" within the large crowd who were true followers of Jesus. To say, *"he opened his mouth,"* was a Hebrew expression of giving a solemn discourse.

Matthew 5:3—*"Blessed are the poor in spirit: for theirs is the kingdom of heaven."*

The two words that are used in the Hebrew scriptures for "blessed" are *baruch* and *ashrei*. The word *ashrei* is used when talking about the blessing that comes on a person who lives righteously; so it is believed this would be the proper Hebrew word. Some modern-day translators use the word "happy," but in Hebrew it means so much more than that. It contains happiness, but it means a conscious peace and protection before the Lord God Almighty, regardless of the circumstances.

To be ***"poor in spirit"*** means to recognize our own spiritual bankruptcy and to cast ourselves on the mercies of God. A full reliance upon God allows the ***"poor in spirit"*** to obtain the kingdom of heaven. So Jesus is not placing a premium on poverty because some are poor because they choose to be poor, but He is referring to the spiritual condition of a person. One day the ***"poor in spirit"*** will be blessed in the future Messianic kingdom that is to come; ***"theirs is the kingdom of heaven,"*** but they are also blessed here and now with God's presence.

Matthew 5:4—*"Blessed are they that mourn: for they shall be comforted."*

This reminds us of the Messianic prophecies like: *"Comfort ye, comfort ye my people, saith your God"* (Isaiah 40:1), *". . . and the days of mourning shall be ended,"* (Isaiah 60:20), and *". . . to comfort all who mourn"* (Isaiah 61:2). The ones who are in God's kingdom will be oppressed by their enemies. This verse may also be referring to the mourning the early Jewish believers would experience as a result of the decline of Israel as a nation. There is a promise in the scriptures that God will one day validate the righteous and punish the wicked. In these strange-seeming paradoxes of the beatitudes, it is not the ones who are mighty and rich who are winning; they just think they are winning.

Matthew 5:5—*"Blessed are the meek: for they shall inherit the earth."*

People who respond to the Messiah in faith, and who rely on God's power, have a sense of humility, gentleness, and meekness. Most of the people who followed Christ in this setting were not able to change their situation with the ruling authorities. They were *"meek"* in the midst of their persecutions. The precious Savior exemplified what true meekness was. Read **Zechariah 9:9 and Matthew 11:29.**

God had promised Israel that one day they would inherit the land. Read **Deuteronomy 11:13–21, Isaiah 57:13, and Zechariah 8:12.** And it seems that Jesus was following many of the verses in **Psalm 37**. But here is the key, only the true Israel would inherit the Land, not just those who could trace their descendants back to Jacob, they had to receive Yeshua in order to be righteous.

Matthew 5:6—*"Blessed are they which do hunger and thirst after righteousness: for they shall be filled."*

A kingdom person will *"hunger and thirst"* after God's righteousness like a person who works to survive physically in this world. When we feed on the Word of God and set our hearts to meditate on God's will for our lives, then we will have a spiritual hunger that will increase. Righteousness is the longing of kingdom person's heart. Read **Psalm 42:1–2, Matthew 18:9–14, and Philippians 3:12.**

"For they shall be filled" brings a real satisfaction knowing that if we seek the Lord, we will find true purpose for our lives. Most of the world knows nothing about true contentment, and they are searching in all of the temporary pleasures trying to find it. God sees to it that His children have true satisfaction when they follow Him. Our circumstances may not always be good, but God is our righteousness; this is the attitude of a kingdom person.

Matthew 5:7—*"Blessed are the merciful: for they shall obtain mercy."*

Why do the kingdom people show mercy, or *chesed* to others? This may be alluding back to **Hosea 6:6**. Because the kingdom people have experienced God's great mercy, they extend that mercy to those around them. This theme occurs throughout the gospel of Matthew with the Messiah showing mercy to others. A person may not meet our personal standards, but that does not give us the right to judge that person. A meek person realizes they are a sinner and they have compassion for others, for they are sinners as well. Jesus condemned the Pharisees of His day for not showing mercy to others (**Matthew 23:23**). The kingdom life is all about relationships with other people. We show others the great love and mercy that God has shown to us through His Son Jesus.

Matthew 5:8—*"Blessed are the pure in heart: for they shall see God."*

The heart, or *leivav,* is the center of all righteous or unrighteous deeds. The heart governs one's actions. A kingdom person will strive for inner purity. A good Old Testament passage is **Psalm 24:3–6**, and a good New Testament passage is **James 4:8**. Lord, that our hearts might be made pure in thy sight!

I think a lot about the people who were so blessed to be able to see the very face of Jesus when He walked this earth (**John 14:9**). And just to think that one day God's children will see His face (**Revelation 22:3–4**). Jesus said that angels see the face of God in **Matthew 18:10**. I love what David said, *"As for me, I will behold thy face in righteousness: I shall be satisfied, when I awake, with thy likeness"* (**Psalm 17:15**).

Matthew 5:9—*"Blessed are the peacemakers: for they shall be called the children of God."*

"Peacemakers" are not passive; they seek to make peace even among their enemies and to reconcile their differences. Since the Messiah is the true Peacemaker (**Psalm 29:11; Isaiah 9:6, 26:12**), those who follow Him will be called *"the children of God."* This does not mean that kingdom people promote peace at any cost; even Jesus knew that He was bringing a certain amount of divisiveness into the world (**Matthew 10:34**). But kingdom people do not seek retaliation; they depart from evil and pursue peace. Many of the bad relationships we face in life may or may not be our own choosing, but we can reflect the peace of Christ in our actions.

Matthew 5:10—*"Blessed are they which are persecuted for righteousness' sake: for theirs is the kingdom of heaven."*

When a kingdom person suffers persecution that comes from a result of doing righteousness, *"for righteousness' sake,"* they shall be blessed.

We should be careful and not confuse this with being persecuted for our own failings in life. Peter talked about this in **1 Peter 3:13–17**; no doubt Peter was reminded of what Jesus said.

"For theirs is the kingdom of heaven" gives the same promise as all the other beatitudes. The kingdom has come into the hearts of the Messiah's people, and one day that kingdom will reach its full realization in the Messianic kingdom. Ishmael will always persecute Isaac (**Galatians 4:29**), and the Daniels of the world are always thrown into the lion's den (**Daniel 6:16**), but God's people will win in the end. What a blessing, that God would even count us worthy to suffer for His name (**Acts 5:41**).

Matthew 5:11–12—*"Blessed are ye, when men shall revile you, and persecute you, and shall say all manner of evil against you falsely, for my sake. Rejoice, and be exceeding glad: for great is your reward in heaven: for so persecuted they the prophets which were before you."*

As animosity grows against Yeshua and His ministry, He seems to be speaking here to His true followers and not the multitude. So what may sound like a redundant statement may be specifically directed to His disciples. As the prophets of old, who took the message of God to the people, were persecuted, and many were killed, so the disciples of Jesus would take His message of the kingdom and would be persecuted, and many would be killed. That persecution would come in the form of slander, insults, and public humiliation. But Jesus told them to *"rejoice."* The disciples would be eyewitnesses of the resurrection of the Messiah, and their powerful witness would be experienced by the pagan Roman world, and consequently persecutions would come. There would be an inner joy from knowing that they obeyed the Lord. Also, when they stood before Christ one day, they would be rewarded for their faithfulness.

So the blessings would come in two ways:

1) Rejoicing, from knowing that they were faithful
2) Rewards, from God knowing their faithfulness

Matthew 5:13—*"Ye are the salt of the earth: but if the salt have lost his savour, wherewith shall it be salted? It is thenceforth good for nothing, but to be cast out, and to be trodden under foot of men."*

Now Jesus moves from the perspective of blessing to the responsibility to live the kingdom life. Historically, salt was gathered from the Dead Sea in Bible times and was used to preserve, purify, and heal. Read **Leviticus 2:13, 2 Kings 2:19–23, and Ezekiel 16:4**. When the salt had lost its *"savor"* and was no longer usable, it was sprinkled on the steps of the temple compound, *"trodden under foot of men"* so the priests would not fall down in the winter months. The disciples were to be salt in a world that was decaying. If they mixed and mingled with the Roman world, they would lose their effectiveness. The Roman world was so immoral, but yet so attractive, and these disciples were to bring the kingdom principles to a pagan world.

Today, we live in a world where all moral standards have been broken down; nothing is sacred anymore. The reason for this is because the followers of Christ have lost their seasoning. They have become like the world around them, and the world has come into the church. As more and more godly believers are taken home to be with the Lord, the world is experiencing what the Bible calls a *"falling away"* (**2 Thessalonians 2:3**).

Matthew 5:14-15—*"Ye are the light of the world. A city that is set on an hill cannot be hid. Neither do men light a candle, and put it under a bushel, but on a candlestick; it giveth light unto all that are in the house."*

Light is a frequent metaphor in the scriptures. Read **Isaiah 42:6, 49:6, 60:3 and Daniel 12:3**. Yeshua the Messiah was the *"true Light"* that came into the world, and His disciples were to be witnesses of that Light (**John 1:4, 8:12, 12:46**).

"A city that is set on an hill" I have talked to many tour guides in Israel, and most of them agree that when Jesus gave this sermon on the Mount of Beatitudes, He was on the northern shore of the lake. He was probably looking across to the eastern shore where the Roman city of Hippos was perched on top of a high mountain. Everyone who lived and worked around the sea could see Hippos day or night. Jesus was using this to tell His followers that there were no secret disciples. The purpose of being a *"light"* is not to hide the light, but to lead others to become disciples as well. The world is a very dark place and we are to be lights shining on the hill.

Matthew 5:16—*"Let your light so shine before men, that they may see your good works, and glorify your Father which is in heaven."*

Here are four aspects of what Jesus was saying to His disciples:

1) They were given the light "your light"
2) They were to let the light shine "before men"
3) Their light would result in "good works"
4) Their good works would glorify the Father in heaven

This was the very message that was laid down in the Torah. Read **Deuteronomy 4:6–8.** The God of Israel is the God of heaven, and He produces a people who are not like the people who worship false gods. His name is to be hallowed and sanctified. We are His family and we represent Him in this present evil world. The very purpose of our lives on this earth is to be in a relationship with the Creator, and others will desire to have that same relationship. This is the kingdom life!

Matthew 5:17—*"Think not that I am come to destroy the law, or the prophets: I am not come to destroy, but to fulfill."*

This verse has been so misunderstood over the centuries because the church has been so far removed from her Jewish roots. Jesus was not saying that all of the Old Testament was nullified by His coming into the world. He certainly fulfilled the law and the prophets concerning His first coming. Read **Luke 24:27, 44**. But the religious establishment of Jesus' time had placed so many man-made fences around the Hebrew scriptures—adding their own oral interpretations—that the Messiah came to establish the law and the prophets in the hearts of His followers. Jesus came to bring back the law's original purpose. Just because all of the sacrificial laws were fulfilled in the Messiah does not mean that the Old Testament is null and void. Jesus was giving a different interpretation of the law than what the people were accustomed to hearing. Many Hebrew scholars believe the Hebrew word for abolish, or *batel*, means to "wrongly interpret." If this be true, then Jesus was saying that He had not come to wrongly interpret the law and the prophets but to rightly interpret the law and the prophets. Notice that the religious leaders accused the apostles in the book of Acts of the same thing (**Acts 6:14**).

Matthew 5:18—*"For verily I say unto you, Till heaven and earth pass, one jot or one tittle shall in no wise pass from the law, till all be fulfilled."*

This verse proves that the Messiah did not come to undermine the law. We are introduced here to a word **"verily,"** or *amein*, that we will see many times in the gospel accounts. It is used as an affirmation of one's own teaching. Many times Jesus will use the words "Amein, amein," which constitutes the certainty of what He is saying. Here Jesus uses the created universe as a standard for God's word. There is a fixed, created order in the universe that demonstrates how God's word must be fulfilled. Read **Psalm 119:89, 89:36–37 and Jeremiah 31:35–36**.

Jesus said, *"one jot or one tittle shall in no wise pass." "Jot,"* or *yod,* means the smallest letter in the Hebrew Aleph-beit. *"Tittle,"* or *keter,* is a small crown or mark on certain letters like the *dalet* or the *resh* that distinguishes them from looking just alike. So to summarize the verse, "the smallest stroke of the smallest letter" will not pass from the law till all be fulfilled. Some people get confused when they see a discrepancy in a Bible translation, but the thing to remember is that the true word of God is without error and is forever settled in heaven.

Matthew 5:19—*"Whosoever therefore shall break one of these least commandments, and shall teach men so, he shall be called the least in the kingdom of heaven: but whosoever shall do and teach them, the same shall be called great in the kingdom of heaven."*

This verse also proves that Jesus did not come to do away with the Law and the Prophets. It is clear when you study the religious Jewish background of Jesus' time, that the rabbis considered some laws of the Torah and the Prophets less important than other laws. For example, one could abstain from eating blood easier than they could honor their father and mother. But Jesus is placing all of the commandments on the same level of importance. If someone breaks one of the so-called least commandments, and teaches others to do the same, their position will be small in the kingdom of heaven (**Matthew 23:23**). But if someone obeys the smallest commandments and teaches others to keep them as well, they shall be great in the kingdom. That there will be different positions in the future kingdom is clear. Read **Matthew 10:41–42, 20:23 and Revelation 22:12.**

Matthew 5:20—*"For I say unto you, That except your righteousness shall exceed the righteousness of the scribes and Pharisees, ye shall in no case enter into the kingdom of heaven."*

The scribes and Pharisees did have righteousness, but they had the wrong kind of righteousness. They went about trying to establish their own righteousness (**Romans 10:3**). The Messiah was the goal of studying the law, and only he could provide divine righteousness. What is so sad as you study the gospel accounts is that the religious leaders had spent so much of their lives studying and learning, but they had neglected the Torah's true teachings. How could this happen? Man's traditions and interpretations of the scriptures blind men from seeing their need of Christ Himself. This is exactly why the Messiah healed on the Sabbath, because the religious leaders were not showing mercy to others; they were worried about looking pious on the outside.

The righteousness that allows a person to enter into the kingdom of heaven is the righteousness that has been provided by faith in the sinless Savior (**Romans 3:21–22**). The Lord Jesus the Christ is our righteousness Yehovah Tisedkenu! (**Jeremiah 23:6, Galatians 2:21**).

Matthew 5:21–22—*"Ye have heard that it was said by them of old time, Thou shalt not kill; and whosoever shall kill shall be in danger of the judgement: But I say unto you, That whosoever is angry with his brother without a cause shall be in danger of the judgment: and whosoever shall say to his brother, Raca, shall be in danger of the council: but whosoever shall say, Thou fool, shall be in danger of hell fire."*[11]

---

[11] When Jesus uses the word "hell," the Hebrew word is *Ge Hinnom*. This Valley of Hinnom runs north and south on the west side of Jerusalem, and east and west on the south side. This word is found seven times in the gospel of Matthew. The Valley of Hinnom was used in **2 Kings 23:10** and **Jeremiah 7:31**, as a place of human sacrifice in idolatrous worship. In later times, the valley was used for burning Jerusalem's trash, and thus constant fires gave a suitable metaphor for a place of God's judgment.

Jesus begins to give a series of antithesis, *"Ye have heard,... But I say unto you."* The term *"ye have heard"* was used to receive a traditional teaching, while *"but I say unto you"* was used to receive the teachings of scripture, and Jesus the Messiah was giving the final word. The religious leaders knew that murder was a heavy law and resulted in death. Read **Exodus 21:12, Leviticus 24:17, and Numbers 35:12**. But Jesus takes it to a deeper level and says that anger is also breaking the law. Anger leads to insult and then to slander, like saying to a brother, *"Raca,"* or "empty headed." Therefore anger has a progression that can lead to murder. A perfect example of this is the story of Cain and Abel. Cain's anger and jealousy led to killing his own brother. Slander is connected to murder in several verses of the Old Testament (**Psalm 31:13; Isaiah 59:3**).

God's counsel is greater than the counsel of the Sanhedrin, and they are hearing from the Messiah the kind of people who are in His kingdom. Kingdom people do not slander their brothers and sisters and try to tear down the character of another individual. Just because the scribes and Pharisees had not committed the very act of murder, did not mean that they were innocent. Their hearts were not filled with love and mercy toward others.

Matthew 5:23–24—*"Therefore if thou bring thy gift to the altar, and there rememberest that thy brother hath ought against thee; Leave there thy gift before the altar, and go thy way; first be reconciled to thy brother, and then come and offer thy gift."*

When a priest was officiating in the temple, he could not tell if the person offering the gift had a repentant heart, but God knew all things. To offer a sacrifice in the Old Testament presupposed a submissive heart to God. A good parallel passage is **Revelation 2:4**, where Jesus knew the intent of the heart was wrong even though their deeds looked good.

The message is clear; God will not accept one's worship while that person is at odds with their brother or sister. Kingdom people come to worship God with a pure heart toward their fellow man. One has to wonder how much of our outward worship is accepted by God.

Matthew 5:25–26—*"Agree with thine adversary quickly, whiles thou art in the way with him; lest at any time the adversary deliver thee to the judge, and the judge deliver thee to the officer, and thou be cast into prison. Verily I say unto thee, Thou shalt by no means come out thence, till thou hast paid the uttermost farthing."*

This scenario is similar to the previous one, but this dispute can only be resolved in court. The wording changes here from a *"brother"* to the *"adversary."* The fact that the judge delivers the person to the *"officer"* and then into *"prison,"* shows that this is not a Jewish court, but a Roman court. So this dispute is between a Jew and the Greco-Roman legal system. What is the point? If a kingdom person lives according to Christ's teachings and is concerned about heaven's courts, then he will never have to face the earth's courts. If a person who is not a believer has a claim against us, we need to make peace as quickly as possible or we will be forced to pay the uttermost. This does not mean that a kingdom person does not stand up for what is right, but the courtroom of Satan can be very unfair and resentful to a child of God.

Matthew 5:27-28—*"Ye have heard that it was said of them of old time, Thou shalt not commit adultery: But I say unto you, That whosoever looketh on a woman to lust after her hath committed adultery with her already in his heart."*

The inward sin of lust can grow into adultery. *"Ye have heard that it was said of them of old time"* may have to deal with the debates that were well known between two rabbis, Shammai and Hillel, in the first century before Christ. One said that only the act of adultery was considered a sin, not the intent of the heart. But Jesus the Messiah disagrees, and says that lust in the heart is also adultery in God's eyes. Kingdom people do not live a life of constant lust in their hearts because this is sinning against one's neighbor and against God Himself.

The sin of adultery was committed by David and it led to murder, even though David did not actually kill Uriah himself. This example shows that David's *"lust"* led to the sins of adultery and murder (**2 Samuel 12**).

Matthew 5:29–30—*"And if thy right eye offend thee, pluck it out, and cast it from thee: for it is profitable for thee that one of thy members should perish, and not that thy whole body should be cast into hell. And if thy right hand offend thee, cut it off, and cast it from thee: for it is profitable for thee that one of thy members should perish, and not that thy whole body should be cast into hell."*

Here Jesus uses the *hyperbole* style of teaching. He is not talking about self-mutilation. Destroying a part of the body does not save anyone from hell. Jesus is saying that purity of the heart is to be considered of greater importance than even the physical life. In Hebrew thought, the *"right eye"* was understood as having a higher importance, and the *"right hand"* was the hand of strength (**Song of Solomon 2:6, 8:3**). Whatever is causing lust in a person's life, they need to get rid of it quickly before it consumes the entire life. Kingdom people have the power to be victorious over the flesh. There is a war between the flesh and the spirit, but through the indwelling Messiah we can be overcomers.

Matthew 5:31–32—*"It hath been said, Whosoever shall put away his wife, let him give her a writing of divorcement: But I say unto you, That whosoever shall put away his wife, saving for the cause of fornication, causeth her to commit adultery: and whosoever shall marry her that is divorced committeth adultery."*

The issue of divorce has caused more spiritual bondage than any other, simply because people have not understood the matter of divorce in the Bible and from the culture in which Jesus lived. The church has been guilty of mistreating many of God's children over the centuries because of ignorance.

The subject of divorce is connected to the previous verses of lust and sexual desires. Selfishness, lust, hatred, and bitterness leads to divorce. Divorce had become very liberal in Jesus' time, and it was very common for a man to divorce his wife if she could not cook well, or if he found a woman who was more beautiful than his wife. Jesus was calling kingdom people back to the sanctity of marriage in **Genesis 2:24**, even though there was a biblical divorce mentioned in **Deuteronomy 24:1**. But it was not clear what was meant if the man found some uncleanness, or *ervat davar,* with his wife to cause the divorce All we know is that it was considered to be a sexual sin of some sort, *"saving for the cause of fornication,"* enough to dissolve the marriage. But how can a married person commit fornication? When a man paid the price for a young girl, called a "dowry," he was paying a large price for her virginity. The marriage was not consummated until they engaged in sexual activity the night of the wedding. The blood-stained sheets were a sign that she was truly a virgin. If there were no blood-stained sheets, the girl had committed fornication before the marriage, and this was grounds for a divorce. Read **Deuteronomy 22:15, 17, 20**.

"Whosoever shall marry her that is divorced committeth adultery." If a man divorced his wife for invalid reasons, the woman was left out in society with no means of providing for herself. So when she remarried, she was committing adultery from a biblical perspective, because the husband had wrongfully divorced her. The whole purpose of a biblical divorce, according to **Deuteronomy 24:1**, was to free the woman to remarry, and the man was not to remarry the woman that he divorced. Divorce dissolved the union completely and gave the right to both persons to remarry. The apostle Paul addressed the matter when a believer was living with a non-believer, and the non-believer decided to leave. A brother or sister was not bond to a marriage if they were deserted **(I Corinthians 7:15)**.

To those who think that divorce is always a sin, they would have a hard time calling God a sinner, because He divorced Israel in **Jeremiah 3:8**, for her harlotry. Even though divorce was certainly not God's will for mankind in the book of Genesis, sin entered into the world and sinful man would make bad choices, and women and children would be abused. Sometimes there is no other way but divorce. Even though this saddens the heart of God, there is forgiveness through Christ and restoration.[12]

To summarize what Jesus was saying, a kingdom person does not take advantage of their spouse. Just because the spouse is not everything they want them to be, they are not to go out and divorce them. Even if there is a biblical reason for divorce, reconciliation is the desirable thing. In a world where the sanctity of marriage has been broken down, kingdom people need to be a witness to the world that love and mercy are not just words; they are to be lived. Kingdom people try to build relationships instead of destroying them. Jesus discusses the matter of divorce further in **Matthew 19**.

---

[12] I have witnessed many cases where the man or the woman was being abused physically and emotionally, and the church condemned the divorced person. I wonder how many people in our churches would be great deacons, Sunday school teachers, and even great pastors, if the church had not wrongfully condemned them. This is not to say that all divorced people are innocent, and that some do not disqualify themselves by their own bad behavior. But when we see the ministry of Christ, He forgave people like the Samaritan woman, who had been married five times and was living with a man. A great revival broke out in Samaria as a result of her talking with the Son of God. We must be careful; God seems to work outside the traditional box most of the time.

Matthew 5:33–37—*"Again, ye have heard that it hath been said by them of old time, Thou shalt not forswear thyself, but shalt perform unto the Lord thine oaths: But I say unto you, Swear not at all; neither by heaven; for it is God's throne: Nor by the earth; for it is his footstool: neither by Jerusalem; for it is the city of the great King. Neither shalt thou swear by thy head, because thou canst not make one hair white or black. But let your communication be Yea, yea; Nay, nay: for whatsoever is more than these cometh of evil."*

Now Jesus takes up the issue of vows and oaths. Normally a vow, or *nadar*, is offered to God, while an oath, or *shava*, is made with one's fellow man. But the two were often used interchangeably. This goes back to **Leviticus 19:12** and **Numbers 30:2**, where they were commanded not to profane the name of the Lord. Like divorce, vows and oaths had become so common in Jesus' time that they had become thoughtless. A person's words had lost their value. Jesus was telling the Jews not to swear by heaven or earth, for they both belong to God (**Isaiah 66:1**). *"Neither by Jerusalem"* because this belongs to God as well; it is His city (**Psalm 48:2**). *"Neither shalt thou swear by thy head,"* for God alone maintains life (**Acts 17:28**). A few years later, James reiterates this thought (**James 5:12**).

Jesus wasn't saying that it was wrong to make a vow or an oath, but he was saying that a kingdom person's word should be good enough.[13]

---

[13] I recall my earthly father, with little or no education, who had very little in worldly possessions because he never made a lot of money in his life. But he could go to the local bank and borrow whatever he needed on just his word. The banker told me one time that he would loan my father anything. My father had integrity, and his word was his bond. How far we have fallen today.

Everything other than our word is superficial and only looks good outwardly to man.

Matthew 5:38-39—*"Ye have heard that it hath been said, An eye for an eye, and a tooth for a tooth: But I say unto you, That ye resist not evil: but whosoever shall smite thee on thy right cheek, turn to him, the other also."*

The law of retaliation is mentioned in **Exodus 21:25, Leviticus 24:19, and Deuteronomy 19:21**. The kingdom law is a higher standard. Jesus seems to be referring to passages like **Psalm 37:1, 8**. We should not render evil for evil, thus having a "get back" attitude toward others. In a world where there is so much jealousy and covetousness, kingdom people who are followers of Christ respond to evil by letting God punish the evildoers. Our example is the Person of Christ Himself (**1 Peter 2:21–23**).

Matthew 5:40-42—*"And if any man will sue thee at the law, and take away thy coat, let him have thy cloke also. And whosoever shall compel thee to go a mile, go with him twain. Give to him that asketh thee, and from him that would borrow of thee turn not thou away."*

Jesus gives three examples of the call for humility and forbearance. In the early first century, many times, all a person had was the inner and outer garments that they wore. If someone had a valid claim against them and sued them for their inner garment, rather than taking some countersuit against the other person, they should give them their outer garment as well. The outer tunic may have been protected under Torah law, **Exodus 22:26–27**, but in this case they were to make full restitution. This would be eliminating further trouble in the case. Kingdom people are to keep down trouble as much as possible, not provoke trouble.

A Roman soldier had the authority to require any common person to assist him in his travels, especially to carry his equipment. The authority could only be extended for one mile. Jesus is saying that the kingdom person should go two miles: *"go with him twain."*

Kingdom people are not to hold such a tight grip on their possessions. If someone wants to borrow something, we should let them borrow it. We are not to hold a grudge against someone because they did not help us in the past. Kingdom people show mercy because God has been so merciful to us, and He supplies our needs. A humble heart is one that gives to others.

Matthew 5:43–44—*"Ye have heard that it hath been said, Thou shalt love thy neighbor, and hate thine enemy. But I say unto you, Love your enemies, bless them that curse you, do good to them that hate you, and pray for the, which despitefully use you, and persecute you."*

In the first century, there were various sects of Jews. There were the secular Jews, who did not believe in God. There were many different sects of religious Jews, including Sadducees, Pharisees, and Essenes, plus the Jews who believed in Jesus as their Messiah. These groups had hatred toward the ones outside of their group, and particularly to the Romans who ruled over them. But instead of showing hatred, they were called by Jesus to go beyond the teachings of **Leviticus 19:18**, and to love everyone. The followers of Jesus were to be different than the rest of the groups.

To *"love your enemies"* was taught in the Torah. Read **Exodus 23:4–5 and Proverbs 25:21**. Kingdom people not only love their enemies, but they *"bless"* them and they *"pray"* for them.

Matthew 5:45—*"That ye may be the children of your Father which is in heaven: for he maketh his sun to rise on the evil and on the good, and sendeth rain on the just and on the unjust."*

Those who are following Yeshua need to strive to be holy as God is holy (**Leviticus 19:2**). God is so filled with love and mercy that He makes

His sun to shine on the evil and He even sends rain on the unjust. This is the attitude of kingdom people. The ungodly farmer may have as good of a crop as the godly farmer. God extends His mercy even to the lost people, hoping that one day they will realize His goodness and turn to Him by faith. We must remember that there was a day when we were lost and God showed His grace to us, and this will help us to extend grace to others.

Matthew 5:46–47—*"For if ye love them which love you, what reward have ye? Do not even the publicans the same? And if ye salute your brethren only, what do ye more than others? Do not even the publicans so?"*

Jesus uses the despised *"publicans"* to get His point across. The overarching lesson that Jesus is conveying to His followers is that one cannot simply extend love to those who love in return. Even a publican can do that. Kingdom people are not to be like the rest of the world, only loving their families and friends who have been nice to them. We are to show the lost world God's love. *"God commendeth his love toward us in that while we were yet sinners, Christ died for us"* (**Romans 5:8**). Even a publican's heart could be changed and become a follower of Jesus, like *Zacchaeus*, whose name means, "innocent or not guilty" in **Luke 19**. Think of Peter loving a tax collector like Matthew. Jesus was preparing these disciples to really make a spiritual difference the rest of their lives.

Matthew 5:48—*"Be ye therefore perfect, even as your Father which is in heaven is perfect."*

The ultimate goal of a person in God's kingdom is to be like God! The cultural and traditional teachings of the Torah had been lowered to fit their own lifestyles (**Matthew 19:20**). But the Messiah came to rightly explain the Torah, and this would guide the people to be more like the Father, not just like other so-called good people.

When we read these kingdom standards, there is no way that we can live up to them, and this is the point. It is impossible without God's presence in our lives. We admit that we cannot live up to these standards, then God forgives us, and we get back in the race again, setting our goal on being like Jesus.

Chapter Six

Matthew 6:1—*"Take heed that ye do not your alms before men, to be seen of them: otherwise ye have no reward of your Father which is in heaven."*

As Jesus continues to give this discourse on the characteristics of people who are in His kingdom, He lays down some practical ways of righteous deeds. In the Jewish mind, there were three things that were considered of prime importance: giving to the poor, praying, and fasting. The emphasis is still on the true righteousness in contrast to the false righteousness of the scribes and Pharisees (**Matthew 5:20**).

"Alms" was a synonym for giving to the poor. The meaning of Jesus' words is clear; if a person gives to others with the motive of being seen of men, there will be no reward forthcoming from the Heavenly Father.

Matthew 6:2—*"Therefore when thou doest thine alms, do not sound a trumpet before thee, as the hypocrites do in the synagogue and in the streets, that they may have glory of men. Verily I say unto you, They have their reward."*

Alfred Edersheim mentions that there were thirteen brass "trumpets" in the Temple, which were containers shaped in the form of a trumpet. *"To sound a trumpet"* was when the noise of the coined money (there was no paper money in Jesus' time) hit the brass trumpets. The difference between the rich and poor casting their coins in the trumpet can be easily seen in the story of the poor widow (**Luke 21:1–4**).

"They have their reward" shows that the hypocrites did, in fact, receive a reward, but that is all they received. Many of the scribes and Pharisees gave their money to be seen and heard, because they loved the praise of men.

Matthew 6:3–4—*"But when thou doest alms, let not thy left hand know what thy right hand doeth: That thine alms may be in secret: and thy Father which seeth in secret himself shall reward thee openly."*

Notice that it was a given for the kingdom people to give alms, *"when thou doest alms."* In the Torah, God told the Israelites to always take care of the poor. Read **Deuteronomy 14 and 15**. *"Let not thy left hand know what thy right hand doeth"* is a Hebrew idiom from **Jonah 4:11**. This meant to give with a sincere heart, even as a child would give. The reward for giving in secret comes directly from the *"Father which seeth in secret himself."*

Matthew 6:5—*"And when thou prayest, thou shalt not be as the hypocrites are: for they love to pray standing in the synagogues and in the corners of the streets, that they may be seen of men: Verily I say unto, They have their reward."*

So much emphasis was placed on the time of prayer or how long the prayer was in Jesus' time. Here, our Lord is telling us that prayers are for the ears of God to hear, not for the eyes of men to see. Jesus has used the term, "hypocrite" several times already. A hypocrite is an impostor—a person who looks good on the outside, but is only wearing a religious mask. The thing that is so disturbing here is that Jesus was talking about many of His own Jewish people. Public praying is not always wrong, but it provides an opportunity for those who love the praise of men. Again, Jesus said, if they pray to be seen and heard of men, there will be no reward forthcoming from the Father.

Matthew 6:6—*"But thou, when thou prayest, enter into thy closet, and when thou hast shut thy door, pray to thy Father which is in secret; and thy Father which seeth in secret shall reward thee openly."*

"Enter into thy closet" is probably a *hyperbole* in order to get the message across to His listeners that private prayer is where there is no pretense; because a private prayer is between the person and God Himself. Jesus is not condemning public prayer; there are plenty of examples of public praying in the book of Acts, but Jesus is giving a warning about the motive of the prayer. I would like to mention six ways that God rewards a sincere prayer:

1) Communion with God
2) God answers the prayer according to His will
3) A deep peace within
4) Stronger faith
5) A clear focus for life
6) Blessed assurance of God's presence

Matthew 6:7–8—*"But when ye pray, use not vain repetitions, as the heathen do: for they think that they shall be heard for their much speaking. Be not ye therefore like unto them: for your Father knoweth what things ye have need of, before ye ask him."*

Here Jesus instructs His followers not to use **"*vain*"** or "meaningless repetitions." It seems to be related to the Aramaic word *battal* meaning "idle, useless." It is similar to our own English word, *babble*. Pagan worship is designed to repeat the same words over and over, hoping to gain the attention of the pagan god, **"*as the heathen do."*** God does not value a prayer based on how many words the prayer contains. God does not need to be informed about anything, **"*for your Father knoweth what things ye have need of, before ye ask him."*** Prayer is not a vehicle to coerce God into action; prayer is intended to know God's greatness and submitting to His will.

Matthew 6:9— *"After this manner therefore pray ye: Our Father which art in heaven, Hallowed be thy name."*

Jesus is not laying down a set prayer, but a model of what constitutes a valid prayer. A genuine prayer should start by praising God's holy name and recognizing His universal rule over the universe.

"Our Father which art in heaven" To know that God is our Father can be taken to be an individual prayer or a corporate prayer. It was common to switch between the singular and the plural. Matthew uses, *"Father Who is in heaven"* thirteen times. What an awesome thought that God is our Father. Read **Romans 8:15 and Galatians 4:6**. Jesus even referred to God as, *"my Father and your Father"* in **John 20:17**. It changes our motive for prayer when we understand that through faith in Christ, God is our Father and we are His children. What amazing love God has for His children! (**1 John 3:1**). We are on the earth and God is in heaven, and yet he hears the prayers of His children.

"Hallowed be thy name" This thought comes from the Hebrew word, *qadash*, thus opening a prayer by recognizing God's holiness and that His Holy Name will be exemplified and honored in our daily lives. In Hebrew thought, to say *"The Name of God"* has nothing to do with a correct pronunciation of His name. Read **Acts 4:12**. To say *"The Name of God"* is indistinguishable from God Himself. Read **Malachi 1:6, Isaiah 29:23, and Ezekiel 36:23**. So many people question God. If God is a just God, then why is there so much injustice in the world? If God is in control, then why do bad things happen to good people? So we should pray asking for God to manifest Himself to the world, reveal Himself in the affairs of men. God's Name is honored by a life of obedience. This was the plan that God had for Israel in **Deuteronomy 4:5–8**.

The true sanctification of God's name is by receiving Jesus as the Messiah, the Son of God. The greatest dishonor of God's name is to reject Jesus as the Son. Read **John 5:22–23**.

Matthew 6:10—*"Thy kingdom come. Thy will be done in earth, as it is in heaven."*

Any blessing that does not mention the kingdom is not regarded as a genuine blessing. The fact that the kingdom is mentioned at the beginning of the prayer shows the importance of this thought. The kingdom of heaven has already arrived in the Person of the Messiah, but has not yet been fully established on the earth. A follower of Jesus in the first century was hoping and praying for the physical kingdom to come in their lifetime. Read **Matthew 19:28** and **Acts 1:6**. Before there were any people called "Christians" (**Acts 11:26)**, those who followed the Son of God were "kingdom people" who focused on God's kingdom in their hearts and the kingdom that was coming. It's sad to hear how many so-called Christian churches do not even preach or believe in a future kingdom. There are over 1,000 references in the scriptures to the future restoration of Israel, mentioned all through the Torah to the book of the Revelation. Jesus said that all of the scriptures must be fulfilled, so how can they be fulfilled without a future kingdom? Even the unbelieving Jew knows that the kingdom is coming; just ask one.

The spreading of the gospel and holy living is hastening the day of the Lord. Read **Matthew 24:14 and 2 Peter 3:11–12**. So when a kingdom person prays, we are to pray for God's kingdom to be enlarged in the hearts of His people, and thus we yearn for His complete rule on the earth. Read **Isaiah 11:9** and **Zechariah 14:9.**

"Thy will be done on earth as it is in heaven." Heaven is a perfect place and God's will is being done there, so our prayer should be that the earth will become a holy place as well (**Isaiah 11:6–9**). Notice the three petitions:

1) That God's name will be honored
2) That God's kingdom will come
3) That God's will would be done on earth as it is in heaven.

Matthew 6:11—*"Give us this day our daily bread."*

Kingdom people are to honor God before we ask Him for anything. And the first request is for food. That the God of Israel feeds the hungry is a recurring theme in the Old Testament. Read **Deuteronomy 8:10, Psalm 107:9, 146:7, and Proverbs 30:8–9**. When Gentiles pray they bless the food, but when Jews pray they praise God for designing the earth to grow the food. Man has not provided the food himself and we should be careful to give God the praise (**Deuteronomy 8:13–14**).

There seems to be a parallel in asking for *"daily bread"* to the manna given to Israel in the wilderness (**Exodus 16:4**). Manna was given in the morning to provide sustenance enough for one day. This also has a strong correlation with the Messiah, for He is the Bread of Life (**John 6:35**). There is a sense of eschatological meaning here as well, for Jesus said, *"Blessed is he that shall eat bread in the kingdom of God"* (**Luke 14:15**).

Matthew 6:12—*"And forgive us our debts, as we forgive our debtors."*

Matthew uses the word *"debts,"* while Luke uses the word *"sins"* (**Luke 11:4**). Matthew was writing to a Jewish audience while Luke was writing to the Greek. The way we can know if we have truly been forgiven of our sins is in our willingness to forgive others. When we hold a grudge or refuse to forgive someone, that is a sign that we have never experienced God's forgiveness. One important way to live our lives toward others is to think forward to the final day when we will stand at the Judgment Seat of Christ. Read **Romans 14:10 and 2 Corinthians 5:10**.

Matthew 6:13a—*"And lead us not into temptation, but deliver us from evil."*

The word *"temptation"* may also be understood as "testing" (**James 1:1–3**). Even though God allows temptations to come into our lives for our own spiritual good, (**1 Corinthians 10:13**; **2 Corinthians 12:7**), we are to pray that He would spare us from those events that bring sorrow and pain. Temptations may come through Satan, our own sinful mistakes, willful disobedience to God, or the result of a sinful, fallen world. But God will always give His children the grace to endure the temptation if we turn to Him by faith.

Matthew 6:13b—*"For thine is the kingdom, and the power, and the glory, for ever. Amen."*

The final line of this verse is not found in any manuscripts dated before the fifth century. Many scholars believe it was added to provide a more liturgical prayer, and not to end the prayer on a negative note. The leader of a congregation would always close the prayer with his own words, and this was believed to have been added later by scribes to Matthew's text. But nevertheless, the thought is well taken, and the basis comes from **1 Chronicles 29:11–13**, in the prayer of David.

Matthew 6:14–15—*"For if ye forgive men their trespasses, your heavenly Father will also forgive you: But if ye forgive not men their trespasses, neither will your Father forgive your trespasses."*

The requirement to forgive others remains a communal setting. It hinders our prayer life when we do not forgive others (**Psalm 66:18**). Again, as the Lord has forgiven us, we are to forgive others (**Colossians 3:12–13**). What does it mean to actually forgive someone? We can gain some insight by studying **Psalm 32:1**: *"Blessed is he whose transgression is forgiven,* or *nasa,* meaning to "lift up," *whose sin is covered."* When we forgive someone we are lifting the weight of guilt from the other person. Biblical forgiveness is not based on waiting for the other person to apologize or to change themselves. We are to forgive the person who has wronged us so that our hearts can be clean from any vengeance of any kind. We must remember that vengeance belongs to the Lord (**Romans 12:17–21**).

Forgiveness is also not based on a restored relationship. We always should desire restoration, but it is not our duty to "get even" or to bring the offender to repentance. The thing that has helped me over the years is to think how God forgave me long before I accepted Christ (**Colossians 2:13–14; Ephesians 2:13**). Jesus died for us long before we were even born. Who are we to harbor unforgiveness toward another person? Bitterness turns a heart to stone. While many have failed to forgive a person who has wronged them in life, bitterness has taken a stronghold in their lives. It is natural thing to sometimes have anger in our hearts toward someone, but that anger does not have to remain there and turn into sin (**Ephesians 4:26–27**). Kingdom people know God's forgiveness; therefore, we forgive those who have sinned against us (**Matthew 5:7**).

Matthew 6:16—*"Moreover when ye fast, be not, as the hypocrites, of a sad countenance: for they disfigure their faces, that they may appear unto men to fast. Verily I say unto you, They have their reward."*

Private fasting is mentioned in the scriptures, as well as corporate fasting. Read **Isaiah 58:3–6; Zechariah 7:5**. It was the custom of the Pharisees to fast on Mondays and Thursdays. Jesus Himself fasted for forty days in **Matthew 4:2**. Fasting and mourning go hand and hand, and this is the reason Jesus said that His disciples need not fast while in His presence; it was a time to rejoice (**Matthew 9:14–15**). One does not gain greater access to God through self-afflicted suffering as the ascetics teach. Nor can one's own suffering affect atoning for one's sins.

But the point that Jesus is making is again that the outward show of the Pharisees was hypocrisy. They put on a sad face in order to not only look pious but to attract compassion from others. The only reward they received was the reward of men. O the blindness of religious hypocrisy.

Matthew 6:17–18— *"But thou, when thou fastest, anoint thine head, and wash thy face; That thou appear not unto men to fast, but unto thy Father which is in secret: and thy Father, which seeth in secret, shall reward thee openly."*

When we fast, we are to appear normal and groom ourselves so others will not know about it. We are so sinful by nature, that even when we are praying properly, we still have the tendency to have a selfish motive in some other area of our lives. True fasting shows a deep desire to know more about God and His will for our lives. We are putting the physical food on a temporary hold, showing to God that we have desired a closer spiritual walk with Him.

Many times Jesus uses the words **"They have their reward . . . the Father will reward thee openly."** Fasting, along with almsgiving and prayer, need to be done *"unto the Lord,"* not for a show to others, lest we lose our rewards.[14]

Matthew 6:19–21— *"Lay not for yourselves treasures upon earth, where moth and rust doth corrupt, and where thieves break through and steal. But lay up for yourselves treasures in heaven, where neither moth nor rust doth corrupt, and where thieves do not break through nor steal: For where your treasure is, there will your heart be also."*

---

[14] I recall a young man who would come to work from time to time looking really down and out, and when asked what the problem was, would say, "Oh, I'm fasting today." Even though I was a new believer at the time, I knew that something was wrong. When another individual I met was fasting you would never know it, and he never mentioned it. His life had the marks of a true follower of Jesus, while the other young man never showed any true spirituality.

Once again, Jesus uses a negative admonition followed by a positive: ***"Do not lay up treasures on earth, but lay your treasures in heaven."*** There are more verses in the gospel accounts concerning the misuse of money than verses about heaven or hell. Even though the scriptures tell us that we are to prepare for the future and provide for our families (**Proverbs 6:6–8, 1 Timothy 5:8**), the problem comes when we spend so much of our time and energy on something that will pass away. Mankind has heard that truth for centuries, but because of the sinfulness of the flesh, we have the tendency to have "money on the brain," just thinking about earthly possessions all the time.

Here, Jesus is telling His followers that treasures on earth can be eaten by moths, and rust can eat them away. James uses the same idea in **James 5:2–3**. Earth is such a sinful place that thieves break in and steal earthly treasures. Homes in biblical times were made out of stone and wood, and many times the people would bury their coins or treasures in a wooden box underneath the floor. And even if the treasures were not eaten by moths or rust, and even if no one stole them, they would be left behind when the person died. The point is that kingdom people need to lay their ***"treasures in heaven,"*** where degenerative forces do not exist.

If a person does not treasure the communion with the Heavenly Father, through faith in His Son Jesus the Christ, then it is certain that they will have the wrong idea about laying treasures in heaven. A person who knows Christ and who is walking in the Spirit, will use their resources for spreading the gospel and helping others along life's way. Read **Luke 16:9–11**. A kingdom person's heart is in heaven, and that's where they lay their treasures because they know they will be safe there.

Matthew 6:22–23—*"The light of the body is the eye: if therefore thine eye be single, thy whole body shall be full of light. But if thine*

eye be evil, thy whole body shall be full of darkness. If therefore the light that is in the be darkness, how great is that darkness!"

Jesus is using the **"eye"** as a metaphor representing the entire person. The true Hebrew understanding of this passage comes from the two idioms, "single or good eye," and "evil eye." The *single eye* is someone who is generous, while the *evil eye* is someone who is stingy. The **"evil eye"** is used in places like: **Deuteronomy 15:9, 28:54; Proverbs 23:6, 28:22.** Kingdom people have an overarching purpose and direction. God has been generous to us, so we are to be generous with those around us. Selfishness is not a mark of a kingdom individual. When a person is existing without the light of God shining in their life, they are in total darkness, but a person who is following the Light of the world is dwelling in His glorious light! One of the great **"I Am"** statements that Jesus made was, *Anee or hah o lam* (Hebrew) "I am the light of the world" (English) **(John 8:12).**

Matthew 6:24—*"No man can serve two masters: for either he will hate the one, and love the other; or else he will hold to the one, and despise the other. Ye cannot serve God and mammon."*

Notice the words **"hate," "love," "hold to,"** and **"despise."** A kingdom person is someone who loves the Lord and their loyalty is to God, not the things of this world. We cannot be a devoted follower of Christ and be divided in our loyalty: *"ye cannot serve God and mammon."* **"Mammon"** can refer to money, property, or possessions. In Jesus' time when someone was serving **"mammon,"** that was considered idolatry.

In our affluent society, many Christians get caught up climbing the economic ladder, and what they do not realize is that it is a trap, and they can never be satisfied. The desire to have wealth just becomes more and more. Their devotion to Christ subsides, and they lose all of their influence as a follower of Christ. Paul would later write that because of the love of money, many have **"erred from the faith"** **(I Timothy 6:10).** Once a person has become used to living on a certain economic level, it is very difficult to return to something modest. I am firmly convinced that in order to live the spirit-filled life that Christ has called us to live, we need to keep our lives as simple as possible.[15] There's not anything sinful about enjoying the fruit of our labor and having nice things, but we have to keep our focus on the eternal things and what our real purpose is on this planet. True happiness comes from knowing Christ and serving Christ. He is our life (**Colossians 3:1–3**).

Matthew 6:25— *"Therefore I say unto you, Take no thought for your life, what ye shall eat, or what shall we drink; nor yet for your body, what ye shall put on. Is not the life more than meat, and the body than raiment?"*

After giving His followers the words about laying their treasures in heaven, then naturally the question might be raised as to how one is to provide for one's own needs. ***"I say unto you"*** shows the authority of Yeshua; His words are not optional. ***"Take no thought"*** is misleading in the English, because Jesus is not saying that we should neglect our needs or

---

[15] There used to be an antique house not far from where we lived. They would buy an entire estate full of furniture and personal possessions after a person had died, and then call us to come over and look at them. Some of the items were priceless to the former owner, like expensive tables, pictures, and jewelry, but now they were being sold to strangers. I had to wonder where the person who left those beautiful material things behind would spend eternity. It was a spiritual lesson for me to see that all that we gather in this life will one day be thrown around by others. May we leave more to our families than just stuff!

the needs of our families. He is saying that we should "not be worried" or "be apprehensive" about those needs. It is a lack of faith to feel anxiety about worldly needs. We have already prayed to the Father to **"give us our daily bread"** (**Matthew 6:11**), so we are to trust that He heard our prayer. The essentials for life are food and clothing, but God knows our needs before we ask Him. He knows how to sustain His children. If we spend all our time worrying about the physical things, then we lose sight of the true meaning of life: **"Is not life <u>more</u> than meat, and the body than raiment?"** Life is made up of more than just food and clothing. Read **Romans 14:17**. We need to focus more on getting more *faith* instead of always getting the needs of the body met.

Matthew 6:26—*"Behold the fowls of the air: for they sow not, neither do they reap, nor gather into barns; yet your heavenly Father feedeth them. Are ye not much better than they?"*

On that spring day in Galilee, when Jesus was giving this powerful sermon, the birds were singing in the trees and flying from limb to limb without a worry in the world. The birds have no occupation; **"for they sow not, neither do they reap, nor gather into barns."** What an example of God's faithfulness! Here Jesus uses the Hebrew style of teaching called *kal v' chomer* or "comparing the lesser to the greater." If the Heavenly Father feeds the birds, *how much more* will He feed His children, who are made in His image?

Matthew 6:27—*"Which of you by taking thought can add one cubit unto his stature?"*

The English word "stature" is misleading when we study verses like **Psalm 39:5** and **Luke 12:26**. Jesus is most likely referring to adding more time to our lives on earth. In other words, worrying and being stressed out about the physical needs of life does not add one more day to our span of life here on earth. Stress and worry can shorten our days on the earth.

Matthew 6:28-30—*"And why take ye thought for raiment? Consider the lilies of the field, how they grow; they toil not, neither do they spin: And yet I say unto you, That even Solomon in all his glory was not arrayed like one of these. Wherefore, if God so clothe the grass of the field, which to day is, and to morrow is cast into the oven, shall he not much more clothe you, O ye of little faith?"*

On the hillsides of Galilee, beautiful, bright flowers start blooming in the month of March. In just a few weeks, the hot sun not only burns the flowers but also burns the green grass. The beautiful lilies and the lush, green grass, is short lived. And Jesus is saying that the flowers that grow wild on the hillsides are more beautiful that the clothing of the world's richest man, Solomon. Once again, Jesus uses the *kal v' chomer* style of teaching, **"shall he not much more clothe you."**

"O ye of little faith." Just because we are in God's kingdom, does not mean that we have great faith. We have placed our God-given faith in Jesus for salvation, but then we are to grow in our faith. It was written of Abraham that he **"grew strong in faith"** (**Romans 4:19–20**). Through studying the scriptures, prayer, assembling with other believers, and doing righteous deeds, we can grow in our faith. Dear reader, how much have you grown in your faith since you have believed in Christ?

Matthew 6:31–32—*"Therefore take no thought, saying, What shall we eat? Or, What shall we drink? Or, Wherewithal shall we be clothed? (For after these things do the Gentiles seek:) for your heavenly Father knoweth that ye have need of all of these things."*

Worrying about things like eating, drinking, and clothing is such a hindrance in our spiritual growth, that Jesus emphasizes them again.

Kingdom people are not to be consumed with these thoughts like *"Gentiles"* or pagans. God has placed us on this earth to know Him and to serve Him. We are to be single minded when it comes to serving our Lord. God desires for His children to enjoy Him and therefore enjoy life at its fullest. Knowing that God loves His children and that He knows everything we need forms the bedrock for the faith we need.

Matthew 6:33—*"But seek ye first the kingdom of God, and his righteousness; and all these things shall be added unto you."*

God's kingdom is comprised of citizens who emulate the righteousness of the King, who is Jesus. When we see His earthly life, He was focused on doing the Father's will, and He did not allow circumstances to take Him away from what He had been sent to do. So the capstone of our Lord's teaching is to *"seek ye first the kingdom of God."* This does not mean that we have to live a life of poverty, or that we will always be rich like many are teaching today. Again, the example is the life of Jesus Himself. He was born in a cave and grew up as a carpenter in a little village called Nazareth. He had His ministry among the common people in Galilee, and many of His followers were the outcasts of His day. He died on a tree for the sins of the world and was buried in a borrowed tomb. Jesus has not only changed our lives, He has changed the course of human history. He chose to live a life of poverty and obscurity in order to show us what our purpose for life really is.

God uses anyone who comes to Him by faith, whether rich or poor. Their social standing does not matter. But if a person is to reach their potential in God's kingdom, their focus has to be on seeking God first and foremost. *"His righteousness"* is not referring to salvation (**Romans 3:22**), but to the character of the people who are following Christ. Remember, the focus here is that the righteousness of the people in God's kingdom exceeds the righteousness of the scribes and the Pharisees (**Matthew 5:20**).

Matthew 6:34—*"Take therefore no thought for the morrow: for the morrow shall take thought for the things of itself. Sufficient unto the day is the evil thereof."*

Tomorrow will have its own anxieties; be concerned about today. Let God take care of the needs of tomorrow. Why worry about tomorrow when we may leave this world before tomorrow gets here? There are many parallels to the Sermon on the Mount and the book of James. James wrote, **"For that ye ought to say, If the Lord will, we shall live, and do this, or that"** (**James 4:15**). This thought also reminds us of a great proverb: **"Boast not thyself or tomorrow, for thou knowest not what another day may bring forth"** (**Proverbs 27:1**).

Thus, the life as a disciple of Jesus, which is life in the kingdom of heaven, is characterized by a growing faith in God. Trusting in the God of Israel through Jesus the Christ means that we live with the kingdom of God and His righteousness as our focus. We don't have to be anxious about temporal needs; we can rest in God's love and power.

Chapter Seven

Matthew 7:1–2—*"Judge not, that ye be not judged. For with what judgment ye judge, ye shall be judged: and with what measure ye mete, it shall be measured to you again."*

As Yeshua continues the Sermon on the Mount, He now talks about how kingdom people are to treat other people. Some have said that this verse forbids all forms of judgment toward others. But this cannot be the case, because Jesus said to *"judge righteous judgment"* in **John 7:24**. There is a time and place to make wise and discerning judgments. Paul said in **Galatians 1:8–9**, *"If any man preach any other gospel unto you than that ye have received, let him be accursed."* In a world filled with false prophets, we must be able to discern who is giving us biblical truth and who is not. So what is Jesus talking about?

Jesus is teaching against a judgmental attitude, placing us in the position of God Himself. We are not to judge our brothers and sisters concerning their salvation or the intent of their hearts.[16] All believers will

---

[16] I knew a man who had a serious disagreement with a local church, and he quit attending church services. He was talked about and judged by many of the church members. But he read the Bible every day, and he gave to the poor in the community without anyone knowing about it. His daily life reflected more the attitude of Jesus than the people who attended church services. We must be careful and not try to place every person in the same box. Many times, God works outside of the traditional standards of

have to stand before the Judgment Seat of Christ (**Romans 14:10**). Kingdom people are to be showing love and mercy to the brethren. If we are judging other people, then God is going to give us the same kind of judgment one day. Some professing Christians are always finding fault with other Christians. We are supposed to be trying to take up for the brethren, not judge them. We are to give people the "benefit of the doubt." When someone has a judgmental attitude, they always presume the worse, but an attitude of love always hopes for the best.

Matthew 7:3–5—*"And why beholdest thou the mote that is in thy brother's eye, but considerest not the beam that is in thine own eye? Or how wilt thou say to thy brother, Let me pull out the mote out of thine eye; and, behold, a beam is in thine own eye? Thou hypocrite, first cast out the beam out of thine own eye; and then shalt thou see clearly to cast out the mote out of thy brother's eye."*

Notice the term, *"brother's eye"*; this shows that Jesus is talking about the community of believers. And there again, there is a time to cast the *"speck"* out of our brother's eye in love, but it is after we have cast the huge *"beam"* out of our own eye. Nothing is more like the Pharisees, or *"hypocrites,"* than for us to reprove someone else when our own life is filled with so many faults. A person who is a chain smoker will have very little effect on telling someone else to quit smoking. It is the oldest sinful

---

our society. I also recall a woman who had lived a very immoral lifestyle for many years. She had lost her credibility with so many people that she had to move away. After many years, the Lord had changed her heart and life and now she is a sincere follower of our Lord. It is not our place to judge others; we should realize that the end of the book has not been written yet.

trick in the world to see the sin in others in order to cover up our own mistakes. When we deal with our own failings in life, the Lord has a way of showing us that the faults of others are not as bad as we thought they were. This was a well-rehearsed topic in rabbinical Judaism in the first century.

Matthew 7:6—*"Give not that which is holy unto the dogs, neither cast ye your pearls before the swine, lest they trample them under their feet, and turn again and rend you."*

We should not disconnect this verse from the previous thought. Just in case someone misunderstood what Jesus was saying, He gives them further instructions about being wise discerners of judgment. Notice the contrasting words *"holy"* and *"pearls,"* compared to *"dog"* and *"swine."* There have been many conjectures over the centuries as to what this verse really means. But the obvious point is that something of high value should not be wasted by giving it to those who neither appreciate it nor use it correctly. The Gospel of the Kingdom is of great value, and the use of the word *"pearl"* is used again in **Matthew 13:45–46**, when Jesus gave the Mysteries of the Kingdom parables. But to say that Jesus is forbidding the giving of the gospel to the Gentiles, as some have said, is contrary to Jesus' teachings (**Matthew 28:19**). Jesus was probably referring to those people who had heard the message and had refused it, or who tried to destroy the message. In the time of Yeshua, the Samaritans were called *"dogs"* and the Romans were called *"swine."* While there certainly were exceptions, like the Samaritan woman in **John 4**, and the Roman centurion who built the Jews a synagogue in **Luke 7:5**, most of them were considered enemies of the gospel. Many of the religious Pharisees and Sadducees were enemies of the gospel as well; however, many did come to faith later on (**Acts 6:7**).

The followers of our Lord were to be wise in their mission of preaching the gospel. They were told by Jesus to *"shake the dust off of their feet"* when the cities rejected the message and go to the next town

(**Matthew 10:14**). Living in a hostile, pagan world, the disciples of Jesus were not to waste much time trying to persuade people to come to Christ whose hearts were hardened to the gospel. Much damage has been done by not realizing the value of the gospel and how it is to be treated. While we are commanded to share with others the precious message of Jesus, we must have discernment about knowing when to share and who to share it with. Only the Lord can change a person's life, and we need to remember that some of the seed that we sow will never bring forth fruit. Zeal is good, but zeal needs to be accompanied with knowledge.

Matthew 7:7-8—*Ask, and it shall be given you; seek, and ye shall find; knock, and it shall be opened unto you: For every one that asketh receiveth; and he that seeketh findeth; and to him that knocketh it shall be opened."*

The teachings of the Sermon on the Mount are difficult, and sometimes they all seem like an impossible task. Forgiving our enemies, forsaking this world's treasures, not having a critical spirit toward others, being good stewards of the message, and not wasting our time, seems impossible at times. So when the kingdom life seems overwhelming, we turn to God in prayer. And the words are **"ask, seek, knock,"** which means to, "keep on asking, keep on seeking" and "keep on knocking." Then the promise is that we will be heard by God. One reason we do not get results in our prayer life is because we ask, wanting something for ourselves instead of wanting to honor God (**James 4:2–3**). We should approach God by being active about it and being sincere about our requests. We have been given an open invitation to come to the throne of mercy, not thinking that we can obligate God to do something for us, but by realizing that whatever we receive comes from His grace and mercy. What a pity, that a kingdom person would neglect the privilege to ask, seek, and knock at the very doorway of heaven!

Matthew 7:9–11—*"Or what man is there of you, whom if his son ask bread, will he give him a stone? Or if he ask a fish, will he give him a serpent? If ye then, being evil, know how to give good gifts unto your children, how much more shall your Father which is in heaven give good things to them that ask him?"*

Matthew uses the *"bread"* and *"fish"* motif possibly for the upcoming miracle of the loaves and fish in **Matthew 14:15–21**. The people of Galilee were well acquainted with the life of an everyday fisherman. One of the ways of fishing was by using as dragnet, by tying weights made out of stones to the bottom edges of the net, thus causing the net to sink all the way to the bottom of the lake. After making a circle with a fishing boat, several men would pull the huge dragnet onto the shore. When emptying the net, they would throw away water snakes, unclean fish (catfish), rocks, and any other objects that had gathered in the net. Only the good fish that had scales would be kept. Jesus was using that background for His teaching about God's goodness. If one of our children were to ask for *"bread,"* we would not give them a *"stone."* Or if one of our children were to ask for a *"fish,"* we would not give them a *"serpent."*

While comparing family relationships, Jesus said that even though we are *"evil,"* we still desire to give good gifts to our children. *"How much more"* shall our Heavenly Father give good things to His children? Once again, Jesus is using the Hebrew style of teaching *kal vy' chomer,* comparing the lesser with the greater. God is such a good God that when we come to faith in Christ, He makes us one of His children. He gives us life eternal, joy and peace for the journey, and then He also provides those everyday needs that we all have. Our job is to believe with all of our heart that God truly loves us and that He desires the very best for us.

Matthew 7:12—*"Therefore all things whatsoever ye would that men should do to you, do ye even so to them: for this is the law and the prophets."*

This has been called the "Golden Rule" and Jesus appears to be putting a "book end" on the Torah and the Prophets, starting back at **Matthew 5:17.** Jewish tradition placed the emphasis on what they were *not to do* against their neighbor, but here Jesus places a positive, ***"do ye even so to them."*** The motivation is not to do good to others hoping for something in return, but in order to honor God's commandments. This goes back to having a ***"pure heart"*** and loving our neighbors as ourselves. I should desire for others to have good health, happy families, and prosperity the same way that I desire those things. Being jealous of the brethren is a wickedness that comes from Satan. There are those who seem to think that if they treat others the way they want to be treated, that this will give them eternal salvation. But remember, the Sermon on the Mount is not the plan of salvation; it is the way a person should live who is following the Son of God. The righteousness of the kingdom people exceeds the righteousness of the scribes and Pharisees. Our focus is on honoring God's kingdom, not honoring ourselves.

Matthew 7:13–14—*"Enter ye in at the straight gate: for wide is the gate, and broad is the way, that leadeth to destruction, and many there be which go in thereat: Because straight is the gate, and narrow is the way, which leadeth unto life, and few there be that find it."*

As a general summary of the Sermon on the Mount, Yeshua now appeals to His disciples to commit themselves to His message. He gives them four warnings, each in a pair:

1) Two gates, two ways (vs.13–14)
2) Two trees (vs.15–20)
3) Two claims (vs.21–23)
4) Two builders (vs.24–27)

The *"wide gate"* is easy to find and that is where the crowd is going to be. The *"straight gate"* is more difficult to find because there are fewer travelers. But the problem is, the wide gate leads to destruction while the straight gate leads to life. The unrighteous go in through the wide gate, because it looks attractive and most people go through that gate. The truly righteous ones enter in through the straight gate, and are not distracted because it only has a few who enter.[17] In the context, the Pharisees and scribes would represent the majority. The ones who chose to follow the Messiah might be the minority in number, but they had heard and obeyed the words of the Master Himself. Even though the straight gate is unpopular, the ones who enter know that it leads to heaven.

Matthew 7:15–20—*"Beware of false prophets,* [18] ***which come to you in sheep's clothing, but inwardly they are ravening wolves. Ye shall know them by their fruits. Do men gather grapes of thorns, or figs of thistles? Even so every good tree bringeth forth good fruit; but a corrupt tree bringeth forth evil fruit. A good tree cannot bring forth evil fruit, neither can a corrupt tree bring forth good fruit. Every tree that bringeth not forth good fruit is hewn down, and cast into the fire. Wherefore by their fruits ye shall know them."***

---

[17] Once I was told by a very godly man of God, "The way that leads to heaven is much more narrow than we have been told." I have to agree.

[18] In Bible times, if a prophet asked for money, he was considered a false prophet. According to what we see on the television these days, there must be a lot of false prophets. Ministry today has turned into big business. The leaders live like kings and queens, and justify taking money from welfare recipients.

Because the wide gate is where the majority of the people will travel, there will be many false prophets drawing them into it. Those who desire to enter into the narrow gate, there will be many false prophets trying to persuade them otherwise. In the first century, there were many false teachers who went around in disguise as having received a special revelation from God. They present themselves as *"sheep,"* but they are really *"wolves."* Jesus uses the backdrop of agriculture to prove His point. The proof of a true prophet is the fruit that they bear. If the prophet brings forth evil fruit, then he is a false prophet. The life has to match what they are preaching or they are false. In the Old Testament, the two things that were a test of a false prophet were:

1) If he led Israel into idolatry
2) If his prophecy did not come true (**Deuteronomy 13:1, 18:20–22**)

So Jesus is telling His disciples to look at the fruit of the prophet. Do their lives conform to the righteous standards of the kingdom? Jesus says that the judgment for a false prophet will result in *"fire."* The judgment will be severe because they led many others into the broad way.

Matthew 7:21–23—*"Not every one that saith unto me, Lord, Lord, shall enter into the kingdom of heaven; but he that doeth the will of my Father which is in heaven. Many will say to be in that day, Lord, Lord, have we not prophesied in thy name? And in thy name have cast out devils? And in thy name done many wonderful works? And then will I profess unto them, I never knew you: depart from me, ye that work iniquity."*

There will be much self-deception among those who are supposedly spiritual leaders. Many of them will think that their good, attention-getting deeds will earn them an entrance into God's kingdom. On the Day of Judgment they will be sadly disappointed. What is so interesting here is that Jesus Himself will be the One who judges them. They were doing good works in His name, but they were impostors, and the King of the kingdom will be their Judge. They called Him ***"Lord, Lord,"*** but they never knew Him as Lord. The thing that is frightening is that it will be ***"many,"*** not just a few. They will appeal the verdict, because they had no idea that they were lost until the end. They lived under a false presumption that their works would save them.[19]

These false prophets will be able to perform miracles, speak prophecies, and perform exorcisms, all in the name of the Lord. By what power are they able to perform these miraculous deeds? Satan! Just as the magicians of Egypt were able to duplicate the miracle of turning a staff into a snake and back to a staff again; just as they were able to duplicate the miracle of turning water into blood (**Exodus 7**).

"I never knew you" This is the difference between a false prophet and follower of Christ. A true follower of Christ ***"knows the Lord, and the Lord knows them."*** It's not just about being able to perform miracles, but it is about truly having a relationship with Jesus. Christ must be formed inside the individual. Dear reader, does Christ know you?

"Depart from me, ye that work iniquity." **Jesus is quoting from Psalm 6:8.** This thought is echoed also in **Matthew 25:41** and **Revelation 20:11, 14.** Jesus will not only decide who enters the kingdom on the Day of Judgment, but who will be banished from His presence. This shows that

---

[19] After the destruction of the temple in 70 AD, the Christian Church started on a downhill journey, moving away from the moral teachings of the Torah. The Christian Church saw the dispersion of the Jews and thought that God was finished with Israel, and the teachings of the Old Testament were outdated. They left their Jewish roots, and created their own Gentile brand of Christianity.

Jesus is none other than God Himself. So the righteousness of kingdom people is not based on deeds that draw amazement from others, but by *walking with Jesus,* which results in loving others the way He does. Kingdom people strive to **"do the will of the Father which is in heaven."**

Jesus spoke these words to an audience who only studied the Old Testament, or the Tanach. This proves that even though Yeshua fulfilled the sacrificial system by His death, burial, and resurrection, and the Temple services, the moral principles of the Torah are still in effect. True, biblical Christianity is to love God with all of our heart, and then to love our neighbor as ourselves (**Deuteronomy 6:5; Leviticus 19:18**). These were written in the Torah years before they were ever written in the New Testament. If a person could do good deeds, *thinking* that they were saved, even in Jesus' day, how much more can we be deceived today? Can church attendance, water baptism, good moral living save us? Of course not, the message is the same today as in Jesus' time; we must **"know Him, and the power of His resurrection"** (Philippians 3:10).

Matthew 7:24–27—**"Therefore whosoever heareth these sayings of mine, and doeth them, I will liken him unto a wise man, which built his house upon a rock: And the rain descended, and the floods came, and the winds blew, and beat upon that house; and it fell not: for it was founded upon a rock. And every one that heareth these sayings of mine, and doeth them not, shall be likened unto a foolish man, which built his house upon the sand: And the rain descended, and the floods came, and the winds blew, and beat upon that house; and it fell: and great was the fall of it."**

This metaphor of a "house standing or not standing" was used in several places in the Old Testament (**Deuteronomy 28:30; Proverbs 10:25, 12:7, 14:11**). As many rabbis in Jesus' day, Jesus concluded the Sermon on the Mount with a *maschal,* or a parable. In the Hebrew language, the word

"hear," or *shema,* means more than just listen; it means "to give attendance to, or to obey." So when Jesus says **"whosoever heareth,"** this carried a much deeper meaning than just intellectual accent.

Both men in the parable are in the "building business." The only difference is the different foundations. One is built on a rock, while the other is built on the sand. The houses in those days were built out of local stone, and if they did not dig down to the bedrock before starting, the winter rains would wash away their house (**Luke 6:48**). Many times, a man was too lazy to dig deeper before starting his house. The spiritual meaning is that one's life can stand on the teachings of Jesus or the teachings of a false prophet. The judgment would not come until the storm came. Both of them thought they would enter into the kingdom. There is a storm coming, my friend, and only those who have built their lives on the Rock of Ages will be able to stand the winds of judgment.

Matthew 7:28–29—*"And it came to pass, when Jesus had ended these sayings, the people were astonished at his doctrine. For he taught them as one having authority, and not as the scribes."*

What was different about the way Jesus taught? The prophets of old would say, "Thus saith the Lord," while Jesus would say, "I say unto you." The rabbis of the day would always quote what another former rabbi had said. Jesus was the Word of God in human flesh! His words were not repetitious or boring; they had life to them. The people had never heard anyone speak like Jesus. His doctrine was different and the way He taught His doctrine was different. The people were filled with wonder and amazement when they heard Jesus speak. His teachings were not just another man's opinion of the day; the teachings of Jesus left the people demanding a decision. Would they follow Jesus or would they refuse? Would they enter into the kingdom or would they not? Jesus presented

Himself within the context of His own teachings, and He left them with the eternal consequences if they refused Him.

There was a sharp contrast between the teachings of the scribes and the teachings of Yeshua. Not only in the way Jesus taught, but by His actions. The religious leaders of the day did not have the love of God in their hearts toward their fellow man. Here comes the Messiah, and the people felt His love when He taught them, and they saw His love in the miracles that He performed. The next chapter begins the healing ministry of the Messiah. His teachings revealed Who He was, and His miracles would further vindicate His claim!

Chapter Eight

In the Hebraic way of thinking, the Messiah had to prove Who He was by His *works*. Up until now, Matthew gives us the *words* of the Messiah, but now he begins to give us His *works*. Read **John 5:36, 10:37–38**. It will be interesting to find that the people who received healing from the hand of the Messiah were either on the margin of the Jewish community, or they were recognized as without public status. There is a leper, a servant of a Roman official, demonized individuals, a paralytic, an unclean woman, the blind, and the deaf and dumb. Even nature itself was under the authority of the Messiah.

The miracles that Jesus performed were clear evidence that He was the Messiah of Israel. The rejection of Yeshua as their Messiah is recorded only after the clear testimony of Who He was. There could be no misunderstanding, and Israel was without excuse.

Matthew 8:1–4— *"When he was come down from the mountain, great multitudes followed him. And, behold, there came a leper and worshipped him, saying, Lord, if thou wilt, thou canst make me clean. And Jesus put forth his hand, and touched him, saying, I will; be thou clean. And immediately his leprosy was cleansed. And Jesus saith unto him, see thou tell no man; but go thy way, shew thyself to the priest, and offer the priest the gift that Moses commanded, for a testimony unto them."*

"When he was come down from the mountain, great multitudes followed him." From the Mount of Beatitudes, you can walk down about

one mile to Capernaum, going east. Even today you can trace the way that Jesus would have traveled when He came down from the mountain. We are reminded of the contrast between the Messiah and Moses. When Moses came down from Mt. Sinai, his face shined so much with the glory of God that it had to be covered (**Exodus 34:29**). When Jesus came down from the Mount of Beatitudes, He did not hide His glory, but revealed Himself through His miracles. He could be touched by the common people. It is no wonder that the multitudes were following Him.

What a wonder, that a ***"leper"*** came to Him on the way to Capernaum. There were two chapters in the Torah (**Leviticus 13, 14**) describing what a leper was to do if they were cleansed. But no Jewish leper had been cleansed since those words were written down, why? Because the Messiah would be the only One who could touch a leper and make him clean.

A leper was considered unclean by the religious Jews, thus emphasizing the broader purpose in the healing ministry of Jesus, making people ***"clean,"*** so they could be a member of His kingdom. The leper did not say "heal me," but ***"Lord, if thou wilt, thou canst make me <u>clean</u>."*** The poor leper was banned from the temple or the synagogue, but he knew Who to worship ***"and worshipped <u>him</u>."*** His plea, ***"Lord, if thou wilt,"*** recognizes Jesus as the Lord of heaven and earth, and also shows that the leper knew Jesus could heal him. The leper also knew the sovereignty of the Lord by saying, ***"if thou wilt."*** Jesus affirms His own sovereign will by saying, ***"I will; be thou clean,"*** not by saying, "as God wills."

"Jesus put forth his hand" The infinitely pure touches the one who is impure. What a demonstration of the love and compassion of Christ, coming to this earth and touching a fallen world. This was His mission!

Jesus told the man to do two things:

1) Tell no man
2) Follow the requirements of the Torah and show himself to the priest and present an offering (Leviticus 13:49, 14:4, 10).

Jesus did not want to start a political revolt prematurely, and He certainly did not want worldly fame. He had to suffer on the cross and rise from the dead to *prove* His messiahship. One of the most interesting things about this miracle is that Jesus intended for the cleansing of the leper to be a ***"testimony"*** unto the priests. If the priests had of been following the true teachings of Moses, they would have known that Jesus was their Messiah. The general unbelief of the religious leaders is woven throughout Matthew's gospel.

Before we leave this Messianic miracle of Jesus, let's gather three thoughts:

1) The <u>pleasure</u> it brought to Jesus to cleanse the leper

2) The <u>joy</u> it brought to the leper to be cleansed

3) The <u>wonder</u> it brought to the multitude

Matthew 8:5–9— *"And when Jesus was entered into Capernaum, there came unto him a centurion, beseeching him, And saying, Lord, my servant lieth at home sick of the palsy, grievously tormented. And Jesus saith unto him, I will come and heal him. The centurion answered and said, Lord, I am not worthy that thou shouldest come under my roof: but speak the word only, and my servant shall be healed. For I am a man under authority, having soldiers under me: and I say to this man, Go, and he goeth; and to another Come, and he cometh; and to my servant, Do this, and he doeth it."*

Here we have a Gentile approaching the Jewish King. Jesus greeted this Gentile with the same ***"I will"*** as He did the leper. It was a good thing for the centurion to be concerned about his servant, but what was even greater was that he came to Jesus with his concern. This appearing of a Gentile parallels the appearances of pious Gentiles from the Old Testament, such as Rahab and Ruth. This foreshadows the wider mission of the Messiah to include the Gentiles in the kingdom (**Isaiah 42:6**).

"And when Jesus was entered into Capernaum" Jesus made Capernaum is hometown, when He left Nazareth (**Matthew 4:13**). Capernaum, "village of comfort," was on the major trade route, the Via Maris, and most likely there was a contingent of Roman soldiers stationed there. ***"There came unto him a centurion."*** A centurion normally was in charge of about 100 soldiers. It's also interesting that a number of centurions are mentioned in the gospels and the book of Acts, and always in a favorable term. Read **Luke 7:5, Mark 15:39, and Acts 10, 27:1**.

Two things stand out about this centurion:

1) His great <u>humility</u>, **"I am not worthy"**
2) His great <u>faith</u>, **"speak the word only"**

The centurion knew that his authority came from Caesar, and he knew that Jesus' authority came from the throne of heaven. If men would come and go at the centurion's command, he knew that disease would fly away at the command of the Messiah. **Psalm 107:20** says, ***"He sent his word, and healed them."*** Matthew is showing that even when Jesus was on the earth, He was still Lord of all!

Matthew 8:10–13—*"When Jesus heard it, he marveled, and said to them that followed, Verily I say unto you, I have not found so great faith, no, not in Israel. And I say unto you, That many shall come from the east and west, and shall sit down with Abraham, and Isaac, and Jacob, in the kingdom of heaven. But the children of the kingdom shall be cast out into outer darkness: there shall be weeping and gnashing of teeth. And Jesus said unto the centurion, Go thy way; and as thou hast believed, so be it done unto thee. And his servant was healed in the selfsame hour."*

"He marveled" What a contrast to **Mark 6:6**, when Jesus marveled at the unbelief of His hometown people, and here He marvels at the faith of a Roman officer. When Jesus said that ***"I have not found so great faith,***

no, not in Israel," He was speaking *"to them that followed."* His own chosen people had not lived up to their calling as the people of God. Read **John 1:10–11**. What made the centurion's faith great? His faith was in the Person of Jesus the Messiah! His great faith also exemplified the fuller meaning of the Abrahamic covenant: *"in thee shall all families of the earth be blessed"* **(Genesis 12:3)**.

"Shall sit down with Abraham, Isaac, and Jacob, in the kingdom of heaven." Jesus is referring to the Messianic banquet (**Matthew 26:29; Luke 14:15**). The Roman officer represented the *"many shall come from the east and west."* There will be Jews and Gentiles who come from the east and the west, but the inclusion in the kingdom will be based on faith in the Messiah, not on social standing or ethnicity. The mention of the Patriarchs of Israel presupposes a resurrection day and the final fulfillment of the Abrahamic covenant. Gentiles will also recline at the table with the Patriarchs of Israel. There is no basis whatsoever for the supersessionist theology here that says that God is through with Israel and all of their promises now belong to the church, or replacement theology.

"But the children of the kingdom shall be cast out" Those Jewish people who fail to receive Yeshua as their Messiah will be cast out; what a sad thought. Sometimes it is the most unlikely ones who will populate the kingdom, and the most likely ones will not. Many Gentiles from far off will come to Christ, and many of His chosen people will go to hell (**Ephesians 2:13**). Many harlots will bow at His feet, while the self-righteous Pharisee rejects His salvation (**Matthew 21:32**).

"Into outer darkness; there shall be weeping and gnashing of teeth" These kinds of designations were common within early Judaism as describing Gehenna, the place where the unrighteous go. The darkness represents a place far removed from God and His light. For the righteous, all weeping ends when they enter into heaven (**Matthew 5:4; Revelation 21:4**), but just the opposite is true for the unrighteous. The chattering of

teeth denotes the lack of peace and the anger that will be in hell. Jesus uses these same words in **Matthew 13:42, 50, 22:13, 24:51, 25:30.**

"Go thy way; as thou hast believed, so be it done unto thee." Another proof of the centurion's great faith was the fact that Jesus told him to go back to his daily life. Go home, and enjoy the fruit of your faith; your servant is healed. What a lesson for us as professing believers! Many times we linger and worry after we have asked the Lord to help us. We need to practice the faith of this centurion. Dear reader, do you have great faith? **(Luke 17:5).**

Matthew 8:14–15—*"And when Jesus was come into Peter's house, he saw his wife's mother laid, and sick of a fever. And he touched her hand, and the fever left her: and she arose, and ministered unto them."*

Archaeologists have confirmed that Peter's house is just a stone's throw from the first-century synagogue. Today, a large Franciscan Church stands over the exact location. It is believed that Peter's house became one of the very first house churches in the first century. It is also probable that Peter's house was a common meeting place for Jesus as well.

This <u>third</u> miracle recorded by Matthew is by the *touch* of Jesus, like the <u>first</u> miracle of the leper was by His *touch*, and the <u>second</u> miracle was by His *word*. This third miracle proves that Peter had a wife. Our Catholic friends say that Peter was the first pope, and they also say that being celibate makes one more godly. We know this is not necessarily true (**1 Corinthians 9:5**). Tradition says that Peter's wife traveled with him on his missionary journeys, and that she suffered martyrdom.

"Sick of a fever, And he touched her hand, and the fever left her" Many scholars believe this may have been malaria. No matter what it was, with one touch from the hand of our precious Lord, the fever was gone. Most of the time when one has recovered from a fever, they are left weak for several days. But the healing was so complete by the hand of Jesus that, *"she arose, and ministered unto them."* What a sight that must have been, seeing Peter's mother-in-law serving Jesus and the apostles. Many women served Jesus in the gospels. Read **Mark 15:41, Luke 8:3, and John 12:2.**

Matthew 8: 16–17—*"When the even was come, they brought unto him many that were possessed with devils: and he cast out the spirits with his word, and healed all that were sick: That it might be fulfilled which was spoken by Esaias the prophet, saying, Himself took our infirmities, and bare our sicknesses."*

The Sabbath had ended, and they began to bring demon-possessed people to Jesus. The streets of Capernaum were filled with sick people. **Mark 1:33** describes the scene: *"all the city was gathered together at the door."* Demons were the agents of disease from a Jewish perspective. The fact that Matthew says that Jesus healed them *"all"* is clearly a foreshadow of the world to come, when all pain will be abolished (**Revelation 21:4**).

"That it might be fulfilled" The scripture that Matthew is referring to is **Isaiah 53:4**. Matthew is making a translation from the Hebrew, not the Greek. Matthew also refers to **Isaiah 53** many times in his gospel: **Isaiah 53:7** in **Matthew 27:12**, **Isaiah 53:9** in **Matthew 27:57**, and **Isaiah 53:10–11** in **Matthew 20:28**. We should therefore seek to interpret **Matthew 8:17** as having a connection to the larger context of **Isaiah 53**.

Again, from the Hebrew perspective, sickness is caused either directly or indirectly by sin. In the Greek mind, there is a vast difference between the physical and the spiritual world, but in the Hebrew mind they are connected. Read **Psalm 25:18** and **Psalm 103:3**. In the larger context of **Isaiah 53**, the manner in which the Messiah bears the sicknesses and sorrows of mankind is through His death on the cross. So our faith in His finished work, not just His earthly ministry, removes our sin and sicknesses.

But Matthew shows a connection between the *healing* ministry of Yeshua and His *death* on the cross, which the Hebrew verbs give Matthew the ability to do that. While using His supreme authority, the Messiah never did so for His own comfort; it was always directed toward the good of others.

Even though physical healing is a benefit of knowing Christ, the final reality of physical healing will not occur until the resurrection, when the believers have a glorified body. So we can't go around thinking that we can tell the Lord what to do and demand physical healing because of the cross, like many try to do. Many times the Lord chooses to not give the physical healing, like in the case of the apostle Paul (**2 Corinthians 12:7–9**). There came a time when the apostles were killed for their faith, and Jesus did not rescue them from death. Contrary to what many believe, sometimes the Lord uses physical weakness to bring about spiritual strength. The physical healing ministry of Jesus vindicated His messiahship and was foreshadowing the future kingdom, when all sicknesses will be erased.

Matthew 8:18–20—*"Now when Jesus saw great multitudes about him, he gave commandment to depart unto the other side. And a certain scribe came, and said unto him, Master, I will follow thee whithersoever thou goest. And Jesus saith unto him, the foxes have holes, and the birds of the air have nests; but the Son of man hath not where to lay his head."*

The healing ministry of Jesus attracted a huge audience: *"great multitudes."* Such authority attracted all kinds of followers. Many modern day, self-made prophets would bathe in the popularity of it all, but not Jesus. He gave the command to depart to the other side of the Sea of Galilee. Jesus would leave a multitude in order to help one or two lost souls. The evangelist Philip left a great revival in Samaria in order to help one Ethiopian eunuch (**Acts 8**).

The answer that Jesus gives to this *"scribe"* shows that His goal was not to just attract a huge following. Jesus knew the heart of the scribe, and He knew if his loyalty was real or not: ***"I will follow thee whithersoever thou goest."*** In the first century, a student would learn from a rabbi—not in a formal classroom, but by following the rabbi.

"Foxes have holes, and the birds of the air have nests" Jesus wanted the scribe to know that following Him was going to take a larger commitment that what he thought. Jesus was on the move constantly, so even the foxes and the birds had more than He did. Jesus had left the conveniences of home, and His ministry was mostly to those who had nothing to give Him in return. The ultimate destination would be the cross in Jerusalem.

"But the Son of man hath not where to lay his head." The title, *"Son of man"* appears first here, and is used eighty-three times in the gospels. This title was not commonly used and was not encumbered by rabbinic sources. You could say that this title was a "clean slate." Jesus uses this to describe Himself. This was clearly a Messianic title from **Daniel 7:13**, while avoiding the term "Messiah." When we look at the entire scope of the title *"Son of man,"* it encompasses two things:

1) The incarnation of the Messiah (**Matthew 8:20**)
2) His divine position, seated at the right hand of God (**Psalm 110:1**)

Matthew 8:21–22—*"And another of his disciples said unto him, Lord, suffer me first to go and bury my father. But Jesus said unto him, follow me; and let the dead bury their dead."*

This *disciple* has a dilemma; he can't go with Jesus to the other side of the lake with regards to his father. It is not clear what the true situation was. His father may have died, and the son wanted to provide a proper burial. Some scholars have said that the father had not actually died and the son needed to stay close by. Others suggest that it was not the initial burial of his father, but the gathering of his bones into an ossuary one year later. Either way, this disciple felt obligated. In the Jewish community, taking care of one's parents in death was considered an utmost priority. Burying the dead was considered a religious obligation based on the fact that God buried Moses (**Deuteronomy 34:6**).

"Follow me; and let the dead bury their dead." On the surface, this sounds like a harsh statement. Most commentators would say that Jesus was saying that even the spiritually dead can take care of the physical dead. But Jesus was using a *hyperbole* like, *"if thy right eye offend thee pluck it out"* in **Matthew 5:29**. Those who are truly consecrated to being His disciple will be thought of as a radical. Even in the face of a difficult situation, we are to follow Christ and trust in His word. The commitment to follow the Son of God is not a normal calling; it exceeds the other important things we are asked to do in life. We see that Jesus had such compassion on those who had lost family members in the gospels (**Matthew 9:24–25; Luke 7:14; John 11:35**). But there is a time and a place for all things, and following Jesus has to be top priority in our lives if we are going to be a good disciple.

Matthew 8:23–27—*"And when he was entered into a ship, his disciples followed him. And, behold, there arose a great tempest in the sea, insomuch that the ship was covered with the waves: but he was asleep. And his disciples came to him, and awoke him, saying, Lord, save us: we perish. And he saith unto them, Why are ye fearful, O ye of little faith? Then he arose, and rebuked the winds and the sea; and there was a great calm. But the men marveled, saying, What manner of man is this, that even the winds and the sea obey him!"*

The narrative picks up from verse 18, where Jesus gave command to depart to the other side, but was interrupted by the approach to Jesus by two of His disciples. "The other side" was a Hebrew idiom for saying,

"Gentile territory," which was the Decapolis. Religious Jews did not go to the "other side"; this was considered an unclean area. Now Matthew shows us that Jesus the Messiah not only had power to heal people, but He also had authority over nature. What a seemingly contradiction! The Messiah has no place to lay His head, but He has the power to control the forces of nature. This is one of the most thought provoking miracles in the gospels, along with Jesus walking on the water, and feeding the multitude. This miracle is one that I always think about when I go to the Sea of Galilee. Matthew is saying to the first-century Jewish followers that this One Who is calling you to be His disciple is not just a common rabbi; He is the Master of the sea.

"He was entered into a ship" In 1985, due to a long drought, the Sea of Galilee was so low that an ancient fishing boat was discovered that dated back to the time of Jesus. It is considered to be the second greatest archaeological find, with the Dead Sea Scrolls being the greatest. It gives us an example of what size boat Jesus may have traveled in. The boat they found was twenty-six feet long and seven and a half feet wide.

"There arose a great tempest in the sea" The Hebrew word for ***"great"*** is *gadol,* which means, "exceedingly great or mighty." This wasn't just a normal storm; it was an earthquake type of a storm, ***"insomuch that the ship was covered with the waves."*** The Sea of Galilee lies 650 feet *below* sea level, and from over 9200 feet *above* sea level, the cold air from Mt. Hermon rushes down through the gorges and ravines. When the cold air starts to twist with the hot air, a storm can happen in just a few minutes. Many Hebrew scholars see this storm as an attempt of the powers of darkness to destroy the Messiah. The sea was a symbol of evil in Jesus' time (**Revelation 21:1**).

"But he was asleep" What a picture! An earthquake-type storm was raging and the Messiah was asleep. We can see His humanity here as much as when He was born in Bethlehem. Jesus was physically spent from the long day of healing in Capernaum (**Matthew 8:1–16**). The fishing boats of that day had a raised section in the stern of the boat, and Jesus may have been underneath the stern on a cushion (**Mark 4:38**). Jesus being asleep also shows the contrast to the disciples being afraid.

"And his disciples came to him, and awoke him, saying, Lord, save us: we perish." Did not Jesus know that there was a storm coming? Of course He did! He was training His disciples in His "classroom" in the actual events of life to teach them genuine faith. These disciples knew the sea very well, and they worked on it all of the time, so their request was not unreasonable. Just because Christ Himself was in the boat, did not prevent the disciples from being tossed by a great storm. Being out in the middle of the Sea of Galilee, in a small boat during a great storm, with water coming into the boat, words come straight and few: ***"save us: we perish."***

"And he saith unto them, Why are ye fearful, O ye of little faith?" What compassion, He spoke to His disciples before He did the storm. Our Lord knew He could calm the storm, but men with ***"little faith"*** needed immediate attention. When Jesus told them they had little faith, He was not saying that they had *no* faith. But that they should exercise greater faith when real tribulations come. He was preparing His disciples for the great troubles that they would face in the near future, taking the gospel into the known world for the first time.

"Then he arose, and rebuked the winds and the sea; and there was a great calm." Wow! I'm reminded of two verses from the Psalms:

"Thou rulest the raging of the sea: when the waves thereof arise, thou stillest them" (**Psalm 89:9**).

"He maketh the storm a calm, so that the waves thereof are still" (**Psalm 107:29**).

There was a "great storm" and Jesus arose from His hard bed and made a "great calm." Not only did the wind stop, but the sea lay down like a piece of glass. As Jesus rebuked the demons, He now rebuked the wind and the sea. The great *Sar Shalom*, "Prince of Peace," speaks peace to the raging sea.

"But the men marveled, saying, What manner of man is this, that even the winds and the sea obey him!" Why did they marvel? How would you feel if you were in a storm on the Galilee, and the Man in your boat talked to the wind and calmed the storm? How would you feel if you knew that God Almighty was in your boat? They were more afraid now than before He calmed the storm. They had come face to face with Elohim, the Creator in the Hebrew scriptures.[20] The God of Israel, Who created everything in **Genesis 1:1**, was defeating the powers of hell. The Lord Jesus Christ, *Yeshua Ha Mashiach*, was the God-Man, Who had come to rescue His people. If Jesus had been only a man, then this would have been reason enough to be amazed, but the fact that He was Man and that He was God really made it a wonder! Matthew is showing that Jesus was identifying with man's limitations, but showing God's authority over Satan and nature itself.

---

[20] So the true meaning of Jesus calming the storm was to show that Jesus was God in human flesh. A ***"greater than Jonah"*** was here (**Matthew 12:41**). The God of Israel was in the midst of His people. We should never downplay the deity of Christ, like many have tried to do. If He can calm the wind and the sea, how much more can He take care of our lives? Just because Jesus is in our boat, that does not mean that we will not go through many storms. But when He says, "let's go over to the other side," He means that *we will make it* to the other side. O that we might have more faith in you, Lord!

Matthew 8:28–29—*"And when he was come to the other side into the country of the Gergesenes, there met him two possessed with devils, coming out of the tombs, exceeding fierce, so that no man might pass by that way. And, behold, they cried out, saying, What have we to do with thee, Jesus, thou Son of God? Art thou come hither to torment us before the time?"*

They came to the country of the *"Gergesenes,"* or *"Gadarenes,"* describing the region controlled by the city of Gadara, near the village of Gergasa, in the land of the Decapolis, or "region of ten cities." Matthew records that *"there met him two possessed with devils,"* while the other gospel writers mention only one. Mark and Luke were writing in singular terms. Like when we say, "I saw Bob Smith the other day," even if more than one person was there. On the hillsides are ancient tombs and caves, which would have provided shelter for these two poor, demon-possessed men. This was clearly an unclean situation. The men were filled with *unclean spirits*, and they had their dwelling among the *unclean tombs*, in an *unclean territory*.

They had driven away everyone else, *"that no man might pass by that way,"* but the demons would be powerless against the power of the Messiah. Just as the storm could have no claim on Christ, neither would the demons.

"What have we to do with thee, Jesus, thou Son of God?" The demons wanted nothing to do with Jesus, but Jesus would have something to do with them. Jesus would give them a taste of what their future state would be: *"Art thou come hither to torment us before the time?"* It's interesting to me, that everywhere our Lord went, the powers of darkness cried out. The devil brought death into the world and the Messiah had come to give life. This proves that the kingdom of God had come, even though the full judgment awaited the end of days. Even demons were not so ignorant of Who Jesus was: *"thou Son of God."*

CHAPTER EIGHT

Matthew 8:30-34—*"And there was a good way off from them an herd of many swine feeding. So the devils besought him, saying, If thou cast us out, suffer us to go into the herd of swine. And he said unto them, Go. And when they were come out, they went into the herd of swine: and, behold, the whole herd of swine ran violently down a steep place into the sea,[21] and perished in the waters. And they that kept them fled, and went their ways into the city, and told every thing, and what was befallen to the possessed of the devils. And, behold, the whole city came out to meet Jesus: and when they saw him, they besought him that he would depart out of their coasts."*

---

[21] Several geo-biologists came to Israel a few years ago. This is the strange and mysterious study of underground demonic activity, or underground terrestrial activity that is evident in and around flowing water. They found a startling discovery. In the place where Jesus came and sent the demons into the herd of swine, they found some of the strongest evidence of terrestrial activity that was occurring in the early first century, similar to what they found at Stonehenge in England. Thus, giving scientific proof that the Galilee was definitely a place of darkness just like the prophet foretold (**Isaiah 9:2; Matthew 4:16**).

In the early 1970s, a road construction crew uncovered a Byzantine Christian monastery and church that dated from the fifth century. It is believed that this church was built nearby where the miracle took place. Just to the south of the Byzantine ruins are the remains of some tombs up on the hillsides where many scholars believe these two men were living when Jesus came to set them free. The modern-day name of the place is *Kursi*, Arabic for "throne."

The gospel of Mark tells us that there were 2,000 pigs, and the name of the demons was Legion (**Mark 5:9, 13**). The fact that there were *"swine"* tells us that this was not a Jewish area; it was a Greek/Roman territory.

"Suffer us to go into the herd of swine" Demons had rather be indwelling pigs than to be in the presence of the Son of God. Demons desire to live inside something or someone.

"And he said unto them, Go" Only a few words to a raging storm: *"peace be still"* (**Mark 4:39**), and only one word to the demons: *"Go."*

"They went into the herd of swine." It's interesting that the Messiah granted their request. They asked for death and that is what they got. The demons thought that by going into the sea, they would be spared some kind of torment. But the swine were killed and so were the demons; they would possess no one else. Luke's gospel says the demons did not want to go into the *deep*, or the *abyss* (**Luke 8:31**). This was the place of the unrighteous dead, the abode of demons, and the anti-Christ himself (**Revelation 20:3**).

"The whole herd of swine ran violently down a steep place into the sea, and perished in the waters." The adjacent hillsides have a rolling effect to them that runs into the eastern side of the Sea of Galilee. With the demons driving the swine, they were doomed for destruction. The fact that Jesus *sent* the demons into the herd of swine showed the two poor men that the demons were gone.

"They besought him that he would depart out of their coasts." The herdsmen who kept the swine went into the city and told them *"every thing"* that had happened. The sad thing is that the people were more concerned about losing their swine than they were the two men being set free. To some men, pigs are more important than souls. The result was not what we might expect. They asked Jesus to leave. One will either run *to* Jesus or run *from* Jesus. There is no middle ground, either we receive Him or

we reject Him. Rejection of the Messiah would not be confined to just His own people; many Gentiles would reject Him as well. Those who accept or reject Jesus do not do so based on their race or social standing, or geographical location. The scriptures do not say, but one has to wonder about the *look* on the faces of the disciples as they started traveling back across the sea. The scriptures never said the disciples got out of the boat. It may be that after their experience out in the storm, they couldn't believe that Jesus was taking them to the "other side."

These two former, demon-possessed men became great witnesses of the power of Christ (**Mark 5:19–20**). Jesus would come back through the Decapolis a few months later, and a great multitude of people would greet Him as a result of these two men spreading the good news about Who Jesus was. In years to come, this region would be Christianized, and some of the bishops who were present at the first Ecumenical Council in the fourth century were from this territory. One reason that these certain miracles are recorded is because the people who met the Son of God face to face made an eternal difference in the lives of others during the first century and later.

Several points of interest are worth mentioning:

1) The devil is real, and demons do exist.
2) We need never fear demons, because they know their destruction is already determined.
3) No one is beyond the saving grace of God.
4) Jesus is the only means by which we can be delivered from Satan.
5) The nearby people were in more serious bondage than metal shackles. They sent away their only hope.
6) In trying to acquire this world's wealth, we can lose our own souls.

Conclusion

We should be reminded that the Holy Spirit guided Matthew to write down specific sayings and miracles of the Messiah, and his book is not intended to be a biography of Jesus. From the genealogy to the birth of the Messiah, to the ministry of John the Baptist, to the announcing of the kingdom of heaven at hand, to calling His disciples, to the Sermon on the Mount, to His miracles, Matthew set the stage to prove that Jesus of Nazareth had to be the long-awaited Messiah of Israel.

We must never forget that these words of Matthew are not mere legends; they are historical facts concerning the Person of the Messiah. God not only gave these words to Matthew, but He preserved these words down through the centuries for His people today.

It is one thing to study and gain more knowledge of Who Jesus is, but these truths must be applied to our daily lives. May we all find the faith and courage to live out what our Lord gives to us. The gospel of the Lord Jesus the Christ is not only truth; it is the power of God!

In Volume Two, we will find the miracles of the Messiah continued, the sending forth of His disciples, Israel's committing the unpardonable sin, followed by Jesus' revealing the mysteries of the kingdom, His rebuke of the religious leaders, the mysterious Transfiguration of the Messiah, and the final words of Jesus before He departed from Galilee.

For additional ministry resources contact:

Carroll Roberson Ministries
203 South Clayton Street
Ripley, Mississippi 38663
1-800-523-3228

www.carrollroberson.com